"*Animal Crisis* is the intellectual sum of two astute thinkers, Alice Crary and Lori Gruen, both powerful leading voices in animal ethics. By deftly weaving tenets and practices of critical social thought with the aims of animal ethics, Crary and Gruen create a new fabric with which to remake human relationships with non-human animals.

The authors do animals the great service of considering them for themselves, of seeing their desires and relationships and experiences, and working to forge a practice that honors that consideration. *Animal Crisis* is a lucid and urgent invitation to a new animal ethics."

Alexandra Horowitz, author of *Our Dogs, Ourselves: The Story of a Singular Bond*

"In this wonderfully thoughtful, elegant, and moving book, two leading philosophers illuminate the contemporary 'animal crisis' that is bringing life on earth to the brink. A vital contribution to the development of 'critical animal theory' as a tool for understanding intersections among different forms of domination, violence, and exploitation that affect humans and other animals alike."

Claire Jean Kim, author of *Dangerous Crossings: Race, Species, and Nature in a Multicultural Age*

"In this powerful book Crary and Gruen insist that we confront the animal crisis that in many ways defines this age of environmental catastrophe. The animal crisis they point to is undoubtedly one of unfathomable loss and damage caused by extinction and climate chaos, but it is also a crisis of thought, solidarity, and political will. At once a foray into the wide-ranging experiences of particular animals attempting to live lives in this crisis, and a philosophical investigation into the need to reinvest animal liberation theory with its social justice roots. *Animal Crisis* offers a path, utilizing an explicitly anticapitalist and antiracist ecofeminism to help guide our way, not to hope, but to action."

Sunaura Taylor, author of *Beasts of Burden: Animal and Disability Liberation*

"*Animal Crisis* presents the reader with the most thorough research into the ways in which animal lives are understood. The arguments are illustrated with stories of individual animals or groups of animals who have been cruelly treated. It is a must for all those who want to understand why we should treat animals ethically."

Dr. Jane Goodall, DBE, Founder of the
Jane Goodall Institute & UN Messenger of Peace

"*Animal Crisis* is a deeply moving book that calls on us to reconsider our relationship to animals and to the other humans and ecosystems we depend on. It offers a paradigm shift, which reveals the ideological distortions that are embedded not only in ordinary life, but throughout philosophical inquiry. It should be read by anyone seeking a way to live and think more meaningfully through our current crises."

Sally Haslanger, author of *Resisting Reality*

"*Animal Crisis* is philosophy as it should be: empirically, socially, and politically informed. This book is so radical, so morally unsettling, that you have to take your courage in both hands to read it. But read it you should. It is that important."

Raimond Gaita, author of *The Philosopher's Dog*

Animal Crisis

Animal Crisis

A new critical theory

Alice Crary and Lori Gruen

polity

First published in 2022 by Polity Press

Polity Press
65 Bridge Street
Cambridge CB2 1UR, UK

Polity Press
101 Station Landing
Suite 300
Medford, MA 02155, USA

ISBN-13: 978-1-5095-4967-2
ISBN-13: 978-1-5095-4968-9 (pb)

A catalogue record for this book is available from the British Library.

Library of Congress Control Number: 2021952119

Typeset in 11 on 15 pt Fournier by
Cheshire Typesetting Ltd, Cuddington, Cheshire
Printed and bound in Great Britain by CPI Group (UK) Ltd, Croydon, CR0 4YY

For further information on Polity, visit our website:
politybooks.com

Contents

About Writing This Book

In the Spring of 2018, we were invited to write an essay reviewing the field of animal ethics. We were both in Princeton at the time, and we met at various cafés and lunch places, trying to find space at little tables for both of our computers. We also met at each other's houses, navigating dogs and children, to make lists and draft strategies. Very quickly we realized it felt more meaningful to devote ourselves to a short, urgent plea to radically rethink animal ethics, both as it is understood in the field of philosophy and as it is taken up and developed within social protest movements. We had each written books and articles urging such a reconsideration in our distinctive ways, and we thought a collaboration would enliven our longstanding commitments to critically interrogate structures that enable the destruction of animals, marginalized humans, and the planet. These commitments were, we found, deepened and, in helpful and illuminating ways, reshaped by our co-writing process.

It is difficult on one's own to write against the grain of received views. Having companionship in the face of intellectual and institutional resistance, as well as global environmental catastrophe, proved to be more than a personal benefit to us, it was also a scholarly and political one. One of the central concerns we each have, and is pivotal in the pages that follow, stems from the belief that attitudes about the world and those who populate it are distorted in devastating ways by ideologies and concomitant material practices that don't aptly capture the value of human lives and relationships, or the value of the lives and relationships of other animals. These distortions permeate standard views in animal ethics, just as they structure many philosophical discussions of social justice. The resulting ideological traps – which appear, at best, as tolerance of, and, at worst, support for, disrespect, commodification, mass violence, and death – must be revealed and challenged if we are to arrive at ethical interventions capable of informing liberating political action. Writing together about the tragic state of the world, during a global pandemic, with a shared recognition of problems at the heart of our current crisis, and a shared desire to acknowledge the dire conditions we all differentially face, has proven to be sustaining. Of course, one cannot change the world alone, but thinking and finding words together is one way of practicing the change we want to see.

Acknowledgments

In writing this book, we drew on a variety of sources –
from academia, from news outlets, from activists, and from
colleagues and friends. Many different animals and their
human defenders have provided us with great inspiration.
We are particularly thankful for the work of the people providing sanctuary for all sorts of animals, including VINE
Sanctuary in Vermont; Foster Parrots/New England Exotic
Wildlife Sanctuary in Rhode Island; and primate sanctuaries
around the world, including those developed in Borneo and
Sumatra for endangered orangutans. Not only do sanctuar-
ies tend to the wellbeing of displaced and rescued animals,
but they provide models for radical multispecies care. We
want to thank Jo-Anne MacArthur and the We Animals
Media team, Anna Boarini of VINE Sanctuary, and Peter
Godfrey-Smith for permission to use their brilliant photographs. We owe thanks for support to the School of Social
Science at the Institute for Advanced Study in Princeton,
Princeton's University Center for Human Values, All Souls
College, Oxford, the New School, and Wesleyan University.
The Brooks Institute for Animal Rights Law and Policy pro-
vided two opportunities for us to work together prior to the
pandemic, and we are grateful for their support as well as for
their work facilitating collaborations.

We are enormously grateful to friends and colleagues who
directly and indirectly contributed to our thinking, including Elan Abrell, Carol Adams, Allison Argo, Jay Bernstein,

Reginald Dwayne Betts, Chris Cuomo, Remy Debes, Cora Diamond, Ann Ferguson, Matthew Garrett, Sally Haslanger, Dale Jamieson, Axelle Karera, Claire Jean Kim, pattrice jones, Justin Marceau, Stephen Mulhall, Timothy Pachirat, Fiona Probyn-Rapsey, Christopher Schlottmann, Amia Srinivasan, Dinesh Wadiwel, and Margot Weiss.

Elan Abrell, Carol Adams, Jay Bernstein, Cora Diamond, Peter Godfrey-Smith, Stephen Mulhall, and Dinesh Wadiwel provided detailed comments on full drafts of the manuscript, as did anonymous readers for Polity, and we are indebted to all of our readers for their astute and gracious engagements with the book. We took all of their comments seriously. Mark Rowlands, who reviewed our proposal for the press, as well as anonymous referees, provided encouraging feedback early on. We presented part of this work at the inaugural meeting of the Harvard–Yale Animal Ethics Faculty Seminar. We thank Lisa Moses for convening the seminar and the participants for thoughtful comments.

Pascal Porcheron has been a wonderful editor, and we are also thankful to Polity's Stephanie Homer and Ellen MacDonald-Kramer for their gracious assistance as well as to Sarah Dancy for her tactful copy-editing. We greatly appreciate Aaron Neber's thoughtfulness in creating an index. We also want to express our gratitude to Gretchen Crary at February Media for her incredible patience, flexibility, and resourcefulness in helping get the word out about this project that means so much to us.

Our families, human and non, have been so patient and accommodating as we wrote. Big thanks to Eli, Louise, Nathaniel, Shepard, Taz, and Zinnia. Our gratitude to them is beyond measure.

Prologue

Human–animal relations are in a crisis of catastrophic proportions. Today it is undeniable that the human use and destruction of animals and their habitats, including practices that result in mass animal deaths, have existential implications not only for nonhuman animals but also for human beings and the planet. This book is written for those who are committed to bringing the crisis clearly into view, with an eye toward envisioning new forms of life that will allow us to build better, life-sustaining relations and act to create a less violent, more caring future.

The academic discipline of animal ethics, which is now roughly 50 years old, has been a key site for discussing ethical interventions into the crisis. We acknowledge the role standard formulations of animal ethics have played in heightening awareness of the predicaments that nonhuman animals confront. These standard views have been informative both in academic contexts and in the larger animal protection movement. But our discussion here has a significant critical dimension.

One prominent strand of animal ethics is preoccupied with animal suffering – suffering that occurs in slaughterhouses, laboratories, and other sites of animal confinement, as well as the suffering that animals experience in the wild. Another prominent strand counters this focus on eliminating suffering, urging that we instead emphasize respect for the rights and dignity of animals. While these strands of animal ethics certainly contribute to increased recognition of nonhuman animals' plights, much of this work obscures, and sometimes even promotes, elements of the crisis we want to resist. The following pages illuminate various ways in which conceptual tools employed within these ethical projects are ill-suited for achieving the goals of genuine liberation.

If we are to address crucial ethical questions about improving our relationships with animals and the existence of all those who live precariously in late capitalism, we need to rethink grounding assumptions of animal ethics as it is currently pursued. Many violent practices are embedded in larger institutions that not only harm animals but serve to disproportionately burden and often subjugate socially vulnerable groups of human beings. Yet the discipline of animal ethics has, to a significant extent, grown up in isolation from traditions of critical social thought that are dedicated to uncovering oppressive structures that impact humans and the more-than-human world. Dominant trends in animal ethics emphasize individual action and overlook damaging social structures and mechanisms of state power, resulting in prescriptions that can serve to sustain these structures and institutions, reproducing the very wrongs they aim to rectify.

Recent attention to political issues that bear on human–animal relations is promising. But even attempts to establish new systems of political rights for animals run the risk of being counterproductive if they don't identify and contest human superiority over animals – human supremacism – that organizes existing political systems. The need for more fundamental interventions into these destructive systems is a theme of some longstanding social and political traditions, including the tradition of ecofeminism.

Ecofeminism, as a theoretical frame and political project, is – like animal ethics – roughly 50 years old. Its assessment of practices that harm and wrong animals is grounded in a multifaceted critique of capitalist modernity. This includes intellectual histories, reaching back to the early modern period, that describe how getting the world in view comes to be understood as requiring dispassionate abstraction. The emergence of this conception of thought coincides both with new forms of devastation of the natural world and with new forms of exploitation of people – primarily women and members of racialized and colonized groups – who do the work of social reproduction. The resulting historical vision, combined with analyses of early capitalist societies, shows how growth and progress are taken to require treating living and nonliving nature as free resources and denying the value of women's and racialized and colonized peoples' care and reproductive labor. This framework enables us to see practices that destroy nature, animals, and marginalized human groups as structurally interrelated, and we are invited to recognize that, in addition to being thus tied together, hierarchical oppositions between human and animal, white and nonwhite, men and women, and primitive and civilized are built into the fabric of capitalist modes of social organization.

A crucial lesson of these analyses is that meaningful steps toward better and more respectful relations with animals must address social mechanisms that also hurt members of human outgroups. When we recognize that distinctions between those deemed human and those considered animals enforce normative rankings constructed partly in tandem with the similarly normatively ordered distinctions among human beings, we can see the urgency of resisting taxonomies that value some in order to disvalue others, and thus relegate so many humans and animals to powerless margins. This recognition positions us to appreciate not only that the categories "human" and "animal" are constructed to pick out, respectively, elites and outgroups, but also that a liberating response will question the legitimacy of the categories that overtly and covertly support violent exclusions. At the same time, it shows us that the reluctance of some contributors to traditional animal ethics to register and resist ways that value-hierarchies animate their thinking ultimately fails animals.

In this book, designed to overcome the social and political isolation of traditional animal ethics, we urge a rethinking of what counts as an ethical intervention. We bring resources from ecofeminism and related critical social theories to bear on the animal crisis, and in so doing we present a new *critical animal theory*. As we develop this new approach, we seek to bring the ideologies and structures of oppression more clearly into view. We also seek to make the lives, experiences, and relationships of other animals visible.

Too often in discussions in animal ethics and politics, animals remain abstractions. We push back against this trend, starting each chapter with a story highlighting animals' experiences, both to show how those experiences matter and to draw connections between the plight of particular animals in particular contexts with the marginalization of humans in those same contexts.

We explore problems of economic inequality and habitat destruction in Indonesia by examining a violent encounter experienced by a mother orangutan in a palm oil plantation. We examine the disposability of both workers and pigs in meat-packing plants and the dangers that they faced during the global pandemic. Through a story of cows and their young who escape their pending demise on small-scale dairies, we illuminate the deep relationships that cows form, while also exploring ways in which some work in animal ethics prevents us from seeing them clearly, or at all. By reflecting on the life and experiences of an octopus, we examine the ways that unfamiliarity and differences in bodies, minds, and evolutionary histories can obscure our understanding of others. One of the most maligned animals, rats, helps us grapple with complexities of thinking through conflicts between human beings and animals, and ways we might develop respect for a very different, perhaps bothersome, other's dignity. A study of captured, traded, caged birds, like parrots, collected for their beauty, reveals how our view of other animals can be distorted in a host of ways, and how such distortions lead to serious harms. Our final case study involves ticks and mosquitos, who are not only in conflict with humans, but whose lives and experiences are particularly challenging to bring into focus. This challenge in many ways parallels the challenge of imagining how to carry on in the midst of the crisis. Thinking simultaneously of the ways that insects are crucial for the sustainability of ecosystems, and of the ways in which some insects also harm humans, is a good route to capturing the role that sensitivity to ecological complexity, and the various conditions of earthly life, must play in envisioning meaningful and timely political resistance.

Throughout the book we work to give animal ethics greater political relevance and traction, in part by highlighting the predicaments of actual animals in crisis. We provide tools for developing a critical political approach to animal ethics that makes it possible to see, and also to act to interrupt, the complex catastrophe currently engulfing all of us, humans and animals.

Figure 1 Orangutans in damaged forest in Indonesia.
Photo courtesy of Ulet Ifansasti/Stringer/Getty Images.

1

Crisis / Orangutans

When members of the Human and Orangutan Conflict Response Unit found a 30-year-old female orangutan in a palm oil plantation near Aceh, in Sumatra, Indonesia, they saw she was in very bad shape. Even those who are accustomed to rescuing endangered orangutans were shocked by what they saw. This lactating mother had been shot with air pellets more than 74 times, both of her eyes were badly damaged, she had multiple broken bones, and she had lacerations from sharp tools or spears all over her body. Her baby was later found in a basket in the nearby village, severely dehydrated and traumatized. As rescuers rushed her and her infant to a veterinary clinic, her baby died. Hope, as the mother is now called, is blind due to her injuries, so she will spend the rest of her life at a sanctuary run by the Sumatran Orangutan Conservation Programme.

The Sumatran Orangutan Conservation Programme, and similar organizations on the islands of Sumatra and Borneo, primarily work to relocate or reintroduce the great apes to protected habitats when they are captured or injured by humans. Direct human conflicts with orangutans have increased over the past several decades as their forest homes have been decimated to create room for palm oil planta-tions. When the orangutans swing into the plantations, they are shot; when they look for food in villages, they are met with violence; and, when a mother is with her baby, people will try to kill her to capture the infant who can be sold on the black market for upward of $20,000.

Wild orangutans live only on these two islands, where they are now critically endangered. The Wildlife Conservation Society describes them as "the rarest of the rare." One species of orangutan in Sumatra, the Tapanuli orangutan, is the most endangered great ape species in the world, with only 800 individuals existing. There are only an estimated 13,800 individual Sumatran orangutans remaining. Both of these populations are in steep decline. On Borneo, it is estimated that the population will be down to 47,000 individuals by 2025. Because a mother orangutan stays with her child for six to nine years, steep population decline is particularly difficult to reverse.

The lush rainforests, home to tens of thousands of species, including the largest carnivorous plants, the largest moths, sun bears, clouded leopards, tigers, gibbons, elephants, and orangutans, are being destroyed at an alarming rate. As Mel White wrote for *National Geographic* in 2008, "considering the island's unsurpassed biodiversity – from orangutans and rhinoceroses to tiny mosses and beetles not yet discovered – and the rate at which its forests are being lost, Borneo's future may well be the most critical conservation issue on our planet." By 2015, the Borneo rhinoceros was considered extinct in the wild. The orangutans on both Borneo and Sumatra may not be far behind.

Three acres of native forests are cut every minute to make room for palm oil monocrop plantations. Forests the size of Connecticut are converted every two years to keep up with the world's insatiable demand for palm oil products. Palm oil is in almost everything, from breakfast items to vegan fare, soaps, cosmetics, shampoo, candies, and snack food. If you look at the ingredients in your cookies, or crackers, or margarine, or peanut butter in your pantry or refrigerator, you will find it listed as palm oil or palm kernel, and most glycerin is from palm oil. Borneo and Sumatra provide 86 percent of the world's supply. In 2019, global consumption was almost 72 million tons, or roughly 20 pounds of palm oil per person. Even those actively seeking to avoid using palm oil find it challenging, as it is ubiquitous and often disguised (Orangutan Alliance).

In order to grow palm trees that produce the large fruits from which palm oil is extracted, native rainforests are bulldozed and then burned. From 2000 to 2015, 150,000 orangutans on Borneo died as their forest homes were destroyed and they became exposed to humans. And orangutans aren't the only creatures to suffer from this massive destruction. In 2015, the fires used to clear the forests burned out of control releasing smoke and ash, severely impacting air quality. Researchers from Columbia and Harvard estimate that this led to 100,000 premature human deaths. The process of cutting down forests, burning what remains, and growing palm trees creates greenhouse gasses, which is ironic given that palm oil is used as a supposedly earth-friendly biofuel. One researcher noted that biofuel production wasn't going to be better for the climate, "instead, it would create nearly double the greenhouse-gas emissions of conventional fuels" (Lustgartner 2018).

With such destructive impact, why would the people of Borneo and Sumatra welcome palm oil plantations to their ecological diverse islands? This question can be partially answered by looking at the history of exploitation of the islands by outsiders. Extraction of wood, animals, and gold by Chinese and Portuguese traders, then British and Dutch colonists, and, more recently, oil drilling by US and European corporations created vast inequalities between native people and multinational corporations and their shareholders. The desire for more direct control and the promise of development has led many local people to join forces with the palm oil industries. But this hasn't always worked out that well. As one report notes:

> To create a legal basis for development, the Indonesian government established a commercial land-share system in the 1980s. In theory, the system let villages sign over development rights in return for some part of the profit. But in practice, many villagers said, companies often secured the permits they needed through some combination of intense lobbying, bribery and strong-arming, and the result was broken promises and missing payments. (Rosner 2018)

Many impoverished villagers view the large orange apes as frightening pests rather than as fellow creatures worth protecting or as indicators of impending environmental collapse. The parents of the young boy who almost killed Hope and caused her infant's death, were resentful that people seemed to care more about the orangutan than their son's future (Beech 2019). But the choice isn't a binary one, nor is it an easy one.

A narrow focus on the desperate straits of orangutans on Sumatra and Borneo – a focus leaving out key features of the larger economic and political context – may very well lead to counterproductive responses and make it seem that consumer boycotts of palm oil are enough to solve the problem. But much more is needed, including a wider critical focus on the destructive logics behind extractive industries to fill out the particular tragedies that befall individuals in their profit-pursuing wake. Multinational corporations have already begun "green-washing" their extractive practices, producing allegedly "sustainable" palm oil, which hasn't helped local people or native animals. We can, and should, care about the orangutans and the villagers who haven't gotten what they envisioned from the corporations that are exploiting land, labor, and animals around them. Sadly, as long as palm oil plantations continue to wreak havoc on Borneo and Sumatra, furthering global inequality, the future of the boy who shot at Hope and her baby, the future of other native children, and the future of the orangutans and other species look bleak.

The Rapidly Expanding Problem

The environmental destruction that is harming the island inhabitants, human and nonhuman, on Borneo and Sumatra represents just a fraction of the unfolding catastrophe around the globe. Human activities are polluting and destroying animal habitats on land and sea at such an astonishing rate that we are confronting a "sixth mass extinction" (Kolbert 2014). Pollution is heating the seas and leaving them strewn with plastic detritus that degrades – as of this writing – nearly 90 percent of the ecosystems of the world's oceans (Jones et al. 2018), while the size and number of fertilizer-laden, run-off-triggered, hypoxic aquatic "dead zones" continue to grow.

The destruction of land-based ecosystems has reached a similar scale and is intensifying. Just as on Borneo and Sumatra, so too the rate of animal-killing forest clearing for agriculture and other human purposes continues to increase in many parts of the world. And animals are being killed at ever higher rates by cataclysms brought on by anthropogenic climate change. It is estimated, for instance, that a billion animals were killed by the fires that scorched Australian landscapes during the first few weeks of the hot season 2019–20 (Rueb and Zaveri 2020). And the fires and unusually high temperatures in the US during the summer of 2021 killed many humans and animals, too, including more than a billion sea creatures (Cecco 2021).

Pollution and human-generated cataclysms haven't spared animals who frequent the skies. Billions of birds have vanished in nearly all areas of North America since the 1970s – a 30 percent loss in overall numbers (Axelson 2019). This silencing of birdsong effectively augurs the "strange stillness" that Rachel Carson ominously and presciently foretold (1962: 110).

The upshot of these interrelated forms of natural devastation is the progressive destruction of life on earth, or ecocide. As environmental reporter Brooke Jarvis (2018) observes:

> What we're losing is not just the diversity part of biodiversity, but the bio part: life in sheer quantity ... the world's largest king penguin colony shrank by 88 percent in 35 years, more than 97 percent of the bluefin tuna that once lived in the ocean are gone. The number of Sophie the Giraffe toys sold in France in a single year is nine times the number of all the giraffes that still live in Africa.

Anthropogenic animal destruction also includes the deliberate creation, exploitation, and killing of animals in laboratories, hunting grounds on land and in the oceans, aqua-farms, and land-based industrial farms. Land-based factory farming alone, increasingly global in its reach, accounts for the slaughter, worldwide, of more than 200 million animals daily (Zamba 2020). The industrialized harvesting of the oceans, taken to encompass industrial fishing and the farming of fish, in turn accounts for the extermination of nearly three trillion creatures annually (Rowland 2017). These technologies of the intentional use and butchering of animals are themselves one of the biggest contributors to the decimation of animal habitats. Worldwide, animal agriculture is a significant contributor to greenhouse gas emissions. The demand for grazing terrain for farmed animals is a major factor in what scientists estimate is the loss of 12.5 million square acres of forests annually (Pearce 2018), which in turn is responsible for nearly 20 percent of the world's greenhouse gas emissions, widespread soil erosion, and related polluting run-off into rivers, lakes, and oceans (Derouin 2019).

The reach of human activity into animal lives and environments is so extensive that it would be difficult to find any unaffected individual animal or animal population. The horrors that human beings visit on animals – incidentally as well as deliberately – are so great and of such massive proportions that, once we begin to bring them into view, we can easily feel disoriented and unable even to properly grasp them. If humans killed each other at the same rate we kill animals, the Humane League has calculated, we'd be extinct in 17 days (@HumaneLeague, July 15, 2018).

These horrors demand an urgent response. Notable political and intellectual pro-animal movements are responding. Their ongoing political interventions are multifarious, including – to give a sense of the range – rescuing animals and human beings from adverse weather events; attempting to slow the devastation of forests and oceans, for instance, by means of Indigenous land defenses and youth climate strikes; agitating for systematic political changes that would shift how humans interact with animals and the environment; helping farmers to transition to plant-based food production; bringing plant-based foods to communities without access to them; and exposing the cruel and callous treatment of animals in concentrated animal feeding operations (CAFOs) and industrial slaughterhouses.

Alongside these and other political interventions are a range of pro-animal intellectual initiatives aimed at establishing the value of animal lives in ways that would account for the felt need for urgent political responses. These intellectual projects are increasingly recognized within the academy. One sign of this is the emerging acceptance of animal ethics within the discipline of philosophy; only 20 years ago it was still a fringe subject represented at best sporadically in Western universities. In addition to becoming a recognized area of study in philosophy departments, animal ethics is taught in other departments in the humanities and the social sciences, in law schools, and in increasingly common animal studies courses and programs. The upsurge of interest in animal ethics as a field is undeniably driven in large part by the recognition that human–animal relations have reached a desperate point. At the same time, embedding the field in the institutional structures of universities risks detaching it from the kind of responsiveness to worldly events that is its original raison d'être. To counteract the scholarly tendency to disconnect from practical matters, here we interrogate received frameworks for doing animal ethics to determine whether their grounding assumptions are genuinely suited for exposing actual harms to animals and the anthropocentric institutions and systems that authorize such harm.

Figure 2 Pigs inside a transport truck heading to slaughter.
Photo courtesy of Jo-Anne McArthur/We Animals Media.

2

Ethics / Pigs

By the middle of spring 2020, the grave risks of exposure to Covid-19 for people living closely with others in the confined spaces of nursing homes and prisons were becoming well known. Given the highly contagious nature of the novel coronavirus, just one positive case often spread to entire indoor populations. Without the possibility of physical distancing, these spaces were dubbed "hotspots" – over 40 percent of deaths caused by the virus occurred in nursing homes, and the rate of infection among prisoners was 5.5 times higher than among the wider US population (Saloner et al. 2020). In April 2020, the concern about hotspots shifted to meat-packing plants where infection rates among workers spiked. Suddenly, places that are usually out of sight, out of mind, were getting more attention than usual. Stories about slaughterhouses and meat-packing plants appeared on the front pages of newspapers and were regularly covered on local and national television news.

The term "meat-packing" glosses over the role played by animals in these plants. During the pandemic, news stories often included photographs of huge, generic warehouse-style buildings containing familiar names like Tyson, or less familiar names like JBS, with small cement statues representing living pigs near the entrances to the buildings. Despite increasing scrutiny of the plants, what happens inside them was left obscure. Animals were generally out of the picture even though they are central to the very purpose of these facilities that quickly slaughter pigs, cows, and chickens and cut them into consumable parts.

Most discussions focused on the conditions that were making the plants' predominantly nonwhite and immigrant workers vulnerable to disease. Workers stand shoulder to shoulder for eight-hour shifts while animals speed by for slaughter, their bodies continuing on, placed on hooks or conveyor belts, to quickly be chopped into pieces. This makes for a dangerous workplace, and long before the pandemic it was well documented that within slaughterhouses the rates of injuries, including fatal ones, are extremely high and, moreover, that meat companies systematically under-reported these harms (Compa 2005; Schlosser 2002; Stauffer 2019). The spread of Covid-19 brought new life-threatening dangers, and, partly prompted by the efforts of Black Lives Matter activists, people started paying particular attention to abuses of nonwhite workers in settings that many had treated as politically unproblematic. It was widely noted that workers were not able to maintain the recommended six feet of physical distance. One commentator observed that "the frenzied pace and grueling physical demands of breaking down so many dead animals can make people breathe hard and have difficulty keeping masks properly positioned on their faces" (Molteni 2020). Others noted that dangers were created by the fact the machinery is noisy and that, to communicate, workers either have to speak loudly, which can increase the spread of the virus, or get close to one another.

The conditions in meat-packing plants are produced by social forces that can be questioned and changed. During the early months of 2020, the fact that the features of the organization of slaughterhouses that put workers at risk are functions of the drive for greater corporate profits received unwonted scrutiny. When conveyer belts carry animal carcasses through slaughterhouses at higher speeds, they "process" more animals and generate greater profits, while at the same time obliging workers to stand closer to each other and work more quickly, putting them at risk of grievous injury. A number of news outlets reported on how, even as it became clear that the virus was spreading swiftly within meat-packing plants, companies were refusing to close down or even to slow down their lines (e.g., Betz et al. 2020; Hughlett and Betz 2020), demonstrating blatant indifference to the health and safety of their own employees.

At one Tyson "pork" plant in Waterloo, Iowa, for instance, 19,500 pigs are killed and made into pork chops and other products every work day – that's 40 pigs every minute. As the virus spiked around Waterloo, health inspectors were called in and found that, though some employees were using bandannas to cover their face, others wore no facial coverings at all. Even after three of the workers tested positive for the virus, adequate PPE (personal protective equipment) was not provided. On April 17, 2020, local officials wrote to Tyson expressing serious worries about community spread of the disease, "especially for the elderly and vulnerable." The plant closed on April 22, and around this time the alleged unwillingness of Tyson to change its operations in the interest of the health of its workers became an object of critical inquiry. One contractor for a different Tyson facility said: "I work around these people every day and could not consciously let them work in an environment where they've been exposed by one person, possibly more and not be told." He was reprimanded for informing Congolese and Mexican workers about positive cases. "I am now worried I will be terminated for reaching out to other human beings. (Something Tyson was not going to do.)" (Telford and Kindy 2020). A pastor from Waterloo said: "What grieves my heart is we have human beings running from war-torn countries, civil wars, ethnic cleansing, human trafficking, running to the United States for a better way of life, only to die as a result of being infected with this COVID virus" (Payne 2020).

Less than a week after the plant closed, then US President Donald Trump declared slaughterhouses part of "critical infrastructure." Within another week, Tyson's Waterloo plant had reopened.

The increased attention the pandemic brought to meat-packing plants, and to the plight of workers in them, did not, for the most part, translate into attention to the animals killed and dismembered on "kill floors." Strikingly, even when public attention turned to what was being done to animals, the emphasis tended to be on the experience of human beings, with animals themselves off stage.

When working at average capacity at all of their facilities, the Tyson corporation kills 155,000 cows, 461,000 pigs, and 45 million chickens *per week*. When a pork plant closes, as the Waterloo plant did for two weeks, the farmers – those who are in the business of intensively breeding and raising pigs for slaughter – have to figure out what to do with the animals who were supposed to be sent to slaughterhouses. The mass production of pigs requires careful timing. Pigs have to reach an optimal weight when they are sent to slaughter: they can't weigh too much or they will be too heavy for workers to slaughter and process; too little weight and there is an economic loss (see Blanchette 2020). As one generation of pigs are sent to the meat-packing plants, youngsters are being fattened up. There are always pigs ready to be killed, pigs that soon will be ready to be killed, and pigs being born to keep the killing and meat-making processes going. The disruption caused by the closing of the slaughterhouses put many producers in positions in which they felt compelled to gas, suffocate, or shoot their animals. The focus of this new reality, though ostensibly about the animals, fell not on the pigs but on the hardship that killing them imposed on pig producers. According to one *New York Times* report, pig farmers in Iowa found it "wrenching" when they had "to kill the animals themselves, and then get rid of the carcasses," one farmer expressing fear that "there would be suicides in rural America." Iowa Senator Chuck Grassley asked the White House's coronavirus taskforce to provide mental health resources to hog farmers, and a pork industry analyst claimed that, while there are immediate economic effects, "the emotional and psychological and spiritual impact of this will have much longer consequences" (Corkery and Yaffe-Bellany 2020).

One way to bring the pigs themselves into view is to reflect on the source of the emotional toll on farmers. Given that these individuals are in the business of raising animals to be killed, why is actually killing the creatures emotionally burdensome? It is implausible to think that the farmers were overwhelmed by the mere idea of "wasting" the pigs that were supposed to feed people. It is more reasonable – and more in line with farmers' own testimonies – to think that, while they could stomach sending animals off to slaughter, they had managed to abstract themselves from concrete details of slaughter, much as the pork-consuming public doesn't want to think too much about the animals that become their ham sandwiches. One farmer who had piglets killed said he didn't want to know how it was done. Another talked about the "emotional strain" of spending a whole day shooting all 3,000 pigs in his barn (Corkery and Yaffe-Bellany 2020).

We have here a particularly striking example of how it is possible to get one's mind around the basic aspects of animal slaughter – as these pig farmers surely have – without registering clearly what is being done to animals. To register the horrors animals endure, we would have to cut through the interwoven physical, social, material, and linguistic practices that keep the actual workings of industrial animal agriculture hidden from view. We would need to see that we have failed to ask about the animals themselves, and we would need to overcome this omission.

In the case of the Tyson pork plant in Waterloo, this would mean turning our attention to pigs, creatures who are as sensitive as dogs and no less intelligent. Pigs are highly social animals who live in small, matriarchal groups. When in more naturalistic environments, pigs regularly interact with each another, huddling and grooming together. They have distinct personalities and develop specific relation-ships. Their social and tactile interactions are a central part of their daily lives in natural settings, where they live up to 15 years. Their confinement on pig farms is frus-trating and stressful, particularly so for breeding sows, and their transport to slaughter is terrifying. In pig production, they are sent to slaughter when they are just six months old. To get in view what is being done to pigs in Waterloo, we would need to get a sense of what individual pigs who were being killed en masse experience before they are slaughtered. We would need to make an effort analogous to what Leo Tolstoy attempted to elicit from readers, when, in the 1890s – and with an eye to exposing the brutality of the pre-industrial slaughtering practices of his time – he described "a well-fed, naked, pink pig being dragged out . . . to be slaughtered":

[The pig] squealed in a dreadful voice, resembling the shriek of a man. Just as we were passing they began to kill it. A man gashed its throat with a knife. The pig squealed still more loudly and piercingly, broke away from the men, and ran off covered with blood. Being near-sighted I did not see all the details. I saw only the human-looking pink body of the pig and heard its desperate squeal; but the carter saw all the details and watched closely. They caught the pig, knocked it down, and finished cutting its throat. When its squeals ceased the carter sighed heavily. "Do men really not have to answer for such things?" he said. (2009 [1883]: 39)

Considering Animals

One of the central conceptual projects that has shaped animal ethics, and also the wider field of environmental philosophy, is laying out why animals should matter morally (Gruen 2017). The project is dedicated to underlining considerations in favor of care and concern for animals that aren't merely instrumental. To be sure, there are good self-interested reasons for human beings to care about what happens to the fauna and flora of the earth – for instance, reasons having to do with the deleterious effects on human individuals and communities from the devastation, displacement, and extinction of species and whole ecological systems. But these are not reasons for believing that animals matter in themselves. Contributions to the field of animal ethics typically start from the idea that there are reasons for concern for other animals that are direct, that is, reasons for concern for the animals themselves, not merely concern owed to human beings.

There are two popular, loosely interrelated ways of going about answering the question, why care about animals? One looks to ethology and physiological studies of animals and aims to show that many animals are similar enough to human beings in relevant respects that they should be brought within the scope of existing moral and legal strictures governing human beings' interactions with each other. Attention to studies of the behavior and physiology of animals, over the last couple of decades, have resulted in enormously widespread scientific agreement that mammals, birds, and fish are conscious and have agency (Jamieson 2018). For example, one often hears that chimpanzees are "so like us" they are "almost human" and that there really isn't a principled way of drawing a clear line between them and us. Indeed, chimpanzees share 97 percent of our DNA, they are socially and emotionally sophisticated, they form strong bonds with their conspecifics and, if they are captive, often with their human caregivers. They are so similar to us – a group of philosophers recently argued – that a powerful case can be made for thinking they merit both moral solicitude and the kinds of protections that human being receive under the law (Andrews et al. 2019).

It would be hard to find anyone working in animal ethics who dismisses as insignificant this growing body of research on animals. It would be equally difficult to find an ethicist who thinks ethological, physiological, or psychological data, even if mightily suggestive, wears its ethical significance on its sleeve. Scientific knowledge, however sophisticated, does not tell us how to treat animals. So, it does not obviate the need to show that animals just are worthy of moral concern.

A second way of showing that animals are deserving of consideration is to focus on the resources that existing ethical traditions have for extending the scope of moral concern to include animals. There is a millennia-long history of moral concern with animals in Western thought (cf. Sorabji 1993), and at different periods moral philosophers have taken an interest in questions about the ethical treatment of animals (cf. Regan and Singer 1989). Looking back only as far as the mid-twentieth century, we find intense public disputes about animal ethics in the Anglophone world that include, to mention just a couple of high-profile interventions, Ruth Harrison's fierce 1964 exposé, *Animal Machines*, which reveals the callous and cruel use of animals in industrial farms, Brigid Brophy's provocative 1965 *Sunday Times* pro-vegetarian article, "The Rights of Animals," and the collection of essays on animal rights, *Animals, Men and Morals: An Inquiry into the Maltreatment of Non-Humans* (Godlovitch et al. 1971). This last book was reviewed in the *New York Review of Books* by Peter Singer, and that project led Singer to write his 1975 bestseller *Animal Liberation*. Singer appeals to a consequentialist doctrine – specifically a form of utilitarianism – that focuses on minimizing suffering, and he develops an argument showing that what human beings do to animals causes tremendous pain and suffering. He concludes that we need to radically improve our treatment of other animals. His argumentative strategy has provided some of the fundamental categories for much work in animal ethics.

Setting aside for a moment an account of how the argument of *Animal Liberation* unfolds – and of how the argument's structure sets the terms for subsequent research – it is worth noting that one of Singer's characteristic gestures in his book is to insist on the reality of animal suffering. It is plausible to think that his book owes its enormous resonance not primarily to its argument, but to its insistence on this point. That might sound like a puzzling claim. Why should we regard it as an achievement to get a broader public to register this reality?

The Reality of Animal Suffering

Most people reading these pages would, if they walked out-side their homes and encountered an injured and struggling dog, cat, bird, or rabbit, unhesitatingly attend to them in a manner that presupposes that the creature is in pain and that they are suffering. Yet there is a sense in which many people who do recognize the reality of animal affliction can also be said to gainsay it. There is a long history of philosoph-ical denial of animal sentience, receiving its most decried expression in the writings of René Descartes, who argued that animals are automata that don't reason or feel pain, and a Cartesian-style image of animals as automata contin-ues to have material repercussions, in advanced industrial societies, in large-scale institutions that treat animals as morally undifferentiated parts of technical processes. For instance, within factory farms today, animals are for the most part treated as, in Harrison's (1964) words, morally insignificant "machines," even though human workers sometimes find themselves forming bonds with the animals they are "processing" (see Ellis 2014). To mention just one other significant case, in laboratories they are more often than not treated as, in Singer's parlance, morally indifferent "tools for research" (2009 [1975]: 25). The coexistence of widespread tolerance of practices that are premised on the denial of animal suffering with equally widespread habits of concern for the suffering of familiar animals may seem to represent a paradox. But there is no paradox. Existing advanced industrial societies are homes to complex webs of social practices that induce in us a "double-think" about ani-mals (Legge 1969). We are brought up in ways that incline us to overlook the tension between taking an immediate interest in the distress of animals close to us and regarding as mostly insensate those whose bodies are consumed as food or dissected in the pursuit of knowledge (see Herzog 2010).

There is a notable body of work by social scientists and social critics interested in animals that describes interlocking physical, legal, social, material, and linguistic practices that keep people from registering what is being done to animals all around them. This failure to attend to what is actually happening fosters internally contradictory modes of thought and conduct. A sizable portion of this corpus is dedicated to describing the web of practices that obscure, in particular, the workings of industrial animal agriculture. At issue are practices that hide the suffering of animals from view, often by shifting attention to the economic process of food production. More than 30 years ago, animal activist and ecofeminist theorist Carol Adams identified and described some of these practices, introducing the term "the absent referent" for the actual animal whose body and experience is rendered invisible (1990: xxv and passim). Adams was concerned with how our talk of "meat" in reference to the tissues of slaughtered animals serves to make the actual animals killed in factory farms disappear linguistically. She was also concerned with how the selling of these tissues in packaging that leaves the original animals unrecognizable amounts to a material erasure of them (1990: 20).

More recently, political theorist Timothy Pachirat (2011) undertook a project in the same spirit, cataloguing the overlapping practices that obscure from view the workings of industrial slaughterhouses. Pachirat takes as his main reference point the case of an Omaha cattle slaughterhouse where he worked for six months, stressing respects in which this slaughterhouse is representative of industrial slaughter in the US. He describes how industrial slaughterhouses, unlike the sprawling stockyards that are their antecedents, are located in out-of-the-way, nondescript buildings and how they are effectively physically hidden. He discusses anti-whistle-blower laws that were passed in several states after the period in which he worked in Omaha – specifically, laws which make it a crime for activists or anyone else to vide-otape, photograph, or otherwise document and share with the public information about what is going on in slaughter-houses. These laws protect the interests of animal agriculture conglomerates. In 2011, journalist Mark Bittman labeled the laws with a catchy and now widely used phrase "ag-gag" legislation – and Pachirat's point in talking about this body of legislation is that it affects the "legal reinforcement of the slaughterhouse's physical isolation" (2011: 7–8). Pachirat tells us that existing social hierarchies contribute to disguis-ing what goes on in industrial slaughterhouses. Today, many of the individuals who are employed on the "kill floors" of these slaughterhouses are members of marginalized racial, immigrant, and economic groups who, while they do indeed sometimes call attention to abuses they witness, are poorly positioned to make sure that the problems are taken seri-ously and addressed.

Echoing Adams's observation, Pachirat recounts how the end products of slaughterhouses are rendered invisi-ble, unrecognizable as once-living beings, through material processes of "manufactur[ing] and construct[ing]" animal bodies "into 'primal' and 'subprimal cuts'" to be wrapped up in cellophane and sold in supermarkets (2011: 30). Further, and again like Adams, he talks about how these end prod-ucts of slaughterhouses are linguistically concealed by name changes. He speaks of "steer to steak" and from "heifer to hamburger" (2011: 45), and, we might well add, "from pig flesh to pork." Novelist and animal activist Jonathan

Safran Foer likewise picks up on this linguistic theme. In his bestselling book *Eating Animals*, he underlines the same kind of verbal masking, explaining that, "when it comes to eating animals, words are as often used to misdirect and camouflage as they are to communicate" (2009: 45).

These thinkers highlight practices that keep the violence of industrial animal agriculture out of the public consciousness. Analogous sets of practices serve to obscure the character of other human enterprises that directly or indirectly harm and kill animals, including the use and killing of animals in laboratories and the destruction of animal bodies and habitats in the clearing of forests to serve human needs. So, it should not surprise us that many people who in some sense cannot help but know that human activity is devastating to animals nonetheless fail to realize that things human beings are doing, even things they are doing on a massive scale, are destroying animal lives. Given the power of these occluding practices, getting the general public to register the reality that human activity is so devastating to animals can be regarded as a significant achievement.

Animal Ideologies

It would be reasonable to speak, in reference to this achievement, of cutting through or unmasking animal-related *ideologies*. This way of speaking fits a familiar conception of ideologies within social thought. "Ideology" is a term for certain ethically loaded beliefs that are integrated into social practices, and, while it is often used as a neutral category in the social sciences, within critical social thought it is frequently taken to be pejorative. What is damaging about ideological beliefs includes an epistemic dimension having to do with how the beliefs distort the nature of the very practices and institutions that they serve to buttress and sustain. The damaging aspect of ideologies also includes a functional dimension having to do with how, in supporting the relevant practices and institutions, they contribute to creating and sustaining relationships of domination. The idea is that, despite their epistemic inadequacy, these beliefs have a practical or material force that lends them an air of truth. In order to liberate ourselves from animal-oriented or other ideologies, we require more than merely intellectual resources; instead, we need material resources and new ways of doing things (see Geuss 1999 [1981]: 5–7).

The practices that serve to keep the workings of industrial animal agriculture hidden are ideologies in this sense. This includes the kinds of specifically linguistic practices discussed by Adams and Pachirat. Describing the end-product of, say, cattle slaughter as "hamburger," instead of as the tissues of dead cows, supports the system of industrial slaughter in part by covering up key aspects of it and thereby making it seem unproblematic. To the extent that beliefs about the eating of "hamburger" support this system, they contribute to the perpetuation of human domination of animals. Moreover, to the extent that these beliefs are integrated into widespread practices of "hamburger" eating – so that it seems unremarkable for the consumption of cow flesh to be part of "happy meals" served to children – they create a world in which eating animals is no big deal, raising no ethical questions at all. One important lesson is that it will take more than an intellectual or linguistic intervention ("that's actually parts of a cow") in order to make the reality of the horrible suffering of animals in industrial agriculture visible. What is needed is a Gestalt switch, an overall change of perspective, of the sort that can be brought about by worldly experiences such as, for example, engagement with literature and other works of art that depict the raw violence of industrial slaughter or that reveal the emotions and relationships that animals have when they aren't under human control; or interaction with individual cows or pigs or animals of other kinds that brings animals into view, say, at an animal sanctuary.

Danielle Celermajer's 2021 book *Summertime: Reflections on a Vanishing Future*, written in response to the devastating Australian brushfires of 2019–20, provides a powerful account of the experiences of pigs and other animals she lives with that helps us shift perspective. Telling us that she cannot grasp "the enormity of the devastation" that the fires brought "not only to humans, but to other wild and domesticated animals," Celermajer sets out to capture the tragedy, not by counting the billions of animal lives lost, but by evoking the toll that the death of one "uncountable" pig, Katy, took on her companion, Jimmy (Celermajer 2021: 12, 58).

Katy and Jimmy were survivors of industrial animal agriculture, having been "discarded as 'wastage'" at three weeks old. Activists scooped them up "tiny and starving, from the factory farm floor where they had been left to die" (Celermajer 2021: 9), and the two were then cared for, protected, and loved by a woman Celermajer calls M, before moving, at four years old – now huge yet timid – to the sanctuary that Celermajer runs with her partner L. Katy and Jimmy remained the closest of companions. In late December 2019, as the fires were threatening their sanctuary, Celermajer and L arranged to have Katy and Jimmy returned temporarily to M. That is when disaster hit. Although the sanctuary remained untouched, "a ferocious fire had enveloped M's place, descending upon them from three sides, razing their home, turning the fields to ash, and killing Katy" (Celermajer 2021: 10), with Jimmy somehow surviving. Celermajer writes about the morning after Jimmy came home:

> He began to look for [Katy]. Everywhere. In their house, down in their woods, up under the trees where they had once taken shade from the afternoon sun. He would turn and look and stand very still – listening for her, perhaps smelling the remnants of her presence. And then he stopped. (2021: 10–11)

For a long time after that Jimmy remained listless. He spoke only in a soft voice as opposed to his regular baritone; he refused his favorite food, watermelon; and he seemed reluctant even to lift his head, lying alone on the bed he and Katy had shared. Celermajer recounts how it required a great deal of patient care before Jimmy gradually returned to some of the joys of life. By telling a portion of Jimmy's story, she gives us a sense of the pathos of one pig's life, his great love and his terrible grief, a glimpse of the immense value and glory that is simply cast aside when a pig is treated as a disposable input to the industrial food system.

Celermajer's narrative does the work of ideology critique, clearing away distortions that tend to obscure our understanding of pigs. She makes the reality of pig life more present and intelligible. Thinkers who contribute to animal ethics don't ordinarily regard either this kind of ideology critique, or the ideology theory that sometimes underlies it, as their purview. But there are a couple of reasons why consideration of ideology is important for animal ethics.

Ideology critique can help us focus on the actual experiences of other animals, in their particular contexts. It can reveal how some significant works in animal ethics owe their undisputed impacts not to the arguments in which they avowedly traffic, but rather to unacknowledged gestures that help to make visible the harms human beings inflict on animals. Singer's acknowledged case against eating animals in *Animal Liberation* is a utilitarian argument that can be stated in plain terms, as we'll discuss in the next chapter. Yet throughout his book we find expressive takes on his stance that, while not part of his official argument, might be seen as getting readers to see in a new and more accurate light the practice of "meat"-eating. For instance, in a late passage in *Animal Liberation*, Singer formulates his opposition to consuming animals in these words: "Flesh taints our meals. Disguise it as we may, the fact remains that the centerpiece of our dinner has come to us from the slaughterhouse, dripping blood" (2009 [1975]: 178). Here Singer calls to our consciousness the animals whose lives are violently extinguished in animal agriculture, thus bringing back for us Adams's "absent referent." Despite the fact that Singer presents himself as predominantly or solely interested in his plain argument for thinking animal suffering matters, he too incorporates literary touches that cut through ideologies that make it difficult to grasp what is done to animals in slaughterhouses.

There is a further respect in which reflection on animal-related ideologies is good preparation for a reconsideration of animal ethics. Even if the critique of these ideologies isn't taken to be part of animal ethics, animal ethicists need to rest on the shoulders of those who do it. If animal ethicists are to speak with authority about how nonhuman animals around us matter, they need to start from the kinds of ideologically undistorted images of animals that ideology critique aims to supply.

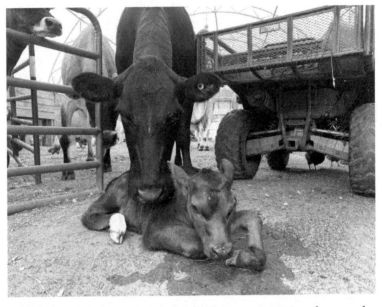

Figure 3 Ebony with hours-old Cora – cows Napoleon and
Magnolia looking on. Photo courtesy of Anna Boarini/VINE
Sanctuary.

3

Suffering / Cows

She may have been pregnant when she escaped. Once in the woods, she gave birth and met up with another cow. Together, the adults kept the infant safe until a local man, who for some unknown reason didn't like the idea that there were cows roaming free in the woods, went out to hunt the trio. He killed her companion. Seeking safety, she and her youngster jumped a fence into an area where there were other cows safely grazing. They were fortunate. The people whose rescued herd they joined didn't want any harm to come to the mother and infant, whom they named Ebony and Ivory. No one came looking for Ebony, but that isn't unusual in the Hudson Valley of New York, where cows often escape from small farms or slaughterhouses. As much as their would-be rescuers would have liked to provide permanent protection for the pair, they were low on barn space, so they worked to find a safe home for this resourceful cow and her child. After spending a couple of weeks getting checked out by Farm Sanctuary in Watkins Glen, New York, Ebony and Ivory were brought to VINE Sanctuary in Vermont, where they will be able to spend the rest of their lives together, free from human threats.

Ebony didn't realize they were safe initially. She was described as being fearful and anxious, in addition to being quite thin as she was nursing a calf and foraging for food. According to pattrice jones, co-founder of VINE Sanctuary, "elder dairy survivor Rose made it her business to soothe and guide the young mother. At first, Ebony hid her son behind a rock wall and did not allow him to leave her side. Within a couple of days, she became comfortable enough to allow the other cows to watch him while she ate or drank" (jones 2019). Having spent months on the run, protecting Ivory and herself from hunters, probably also mourning the loss of her companion, fiercely protective Ebony slowly but surely began to settle in with her new cow community.

Ebony may very well have escaped so she could keep her calf. It is not cost-effective to allow infants to nurse from their mothers, as milk production for humans is the point of the dairy business. Female calves are usually bottle fed and become replacement milk cows. Male calves, like Ivory, are considered surplus. It used to be profitable for dairy farmers to send them to veal production facilities, but since the demand for veal has dropped as more and more people have learned of the cruelty involved in keeping baby cows chained so their muscles remain tender before killing them, it isn't cost-effective to pay for transport. Now, many dairy farms kill the male infants, what is known as the industry's "dirty little secret" (Levitt 2018). Some smaller farmers let the male infants starve. One of the smaller, bio-organic farmers is of the view that "if you eat dairy the responsible thing to do is eat some veal too. Every year a cow has a calf in order to keep the milk flowing. About half of these calves are bull calves."

It would be hard to deny both Ebony's interest in freedom and her very strong interest in staying with her infant. Nonetheless, dairy farmers ignore these interests. Not long after Ebony and Ivory arrived at VINE Sanctuary, another cow, named Norma, and her daughter, Nina, arrived. Norma and Nina hadn't liberated themselves from a farm. Instead, a human, from a hospital bed, had urged that they be sent to sanctuary. Norma had used her horns to protect her newborn calf and had injured the farm worker who was trying to take Nina away. Because Norma had injured a worker previously, the small biodynamic dairy was going to send her to slaughter. The injured worker, who needed stiches, urged that Norma be allowed to go to sanctuary, and VINE was also able to bring Nina. Norma, like Ebony, did what she could to avoid being separated from her child.

That these cows have an interest in being with their offspring should not be surprising. There are many news stories of cows running after trucks taking their calves away and other stories of dairy farmers admitting that mothers and infants cry for days after separation. One study found that calves experience emotional pain when separated from their mothers, which can lead them to stop eating and suffer a type of "negative cognitive bias similar to pessimism" (Bates 2014). This type of emotional suffering raises questions about the very possibility of "humane" dairy farming.

Norma and Nina were living on a so-called "humane" dairy farm. Churchtown Dairy is a small farm in the Hudson Valley, not too far from where Ebony and Ivory were found, that prides itself on creating "ethically produced cheeses" by working "with the milk to identify its strengths and weaknesses, what styles it is well suited for, and work with the farm team to optimize handling and treatment of the milk to maximize quality." Presumably they also display the same attentive care for the cows from whom the milk is taken. The cows are milked twice a day, sometimes by hand and sometimes by machine. They live in a spacious barn in the winter and roam the pastures in the spring and summer. This farm allowed Nina to stay with her mother for longer than the few hours that is typical on most dairy farms. Nina would have become a dairy producer herself.

From a utilitarian point of view, given that Norma was relatively happy and given that Nina could replace her in making the milk that would lead to people's "compassionate" enjoyment of carefully crafted cheese and raw milk, it would have been fine for the farm to send Norma to slaughter. As long as people take pleasure in consuming these products, and as long as Norma was treated relatively well, and was killed relatively painlessly, then, from the utilitarian point of view of the universe, her death wouldn't be objectionable. As long as the total amount of happiness stays the same, for utilitarians it doesn't matter who is experiencing that happiness. As utilitarian philosopher Henry Sidgwick urged, we should consider the good of any one individual as equivalent to the good of any other. So, on a utilitarian account, if Norma was painlessly slaughtered and Nina experienced the same general amount of contentment, then there would be no loss in utility and thus nothing wrong. Some might even argue that the money that will be spent to care for Norma for the rest of her life in sanctuary could be more effectively used raising awareness about the harms caused by industrial animal farming. Killing Norma, all things considered, may have been better, from a utilitarian perspective, than keeping her and Nina at the sanctuary.

One of the criticisms that utilitarians face is that their theories allow them to readily condone the death of Norma as long as there is another cow that was brought into existence who would, over her life, have roughly the same amount of utility. In fact, many of the small, biodynamic "humane" farms adopt something very much like this utilitarian reasoning. Cows, calves, and, on some versions of consequentialism (the larger theory that utilitarianism fall under), even humans don't matter in themselves, they are just vessels of value. If you can create another vessel, then it isn't wrong to destroy the current one, especially if the destruction causes little or no suffering. This is sometimes referred to as the "replaceability argument." Some consequentialists have argued that it is not simply acceptable, but right to kill someone, if another being can be brought into existence who would otherwise not experience anything. As R.M. Hare wrote: "For it is better for an animal to have a happy life, even if it is a short one, than no life at all" (Hare 1999: 239).

Consequentialists embrace counterintuitive conclusions when it comes to killing. Many people become vegetarians because they are opposed to killing animals to eat them, and many people become vegan because, even though dairy cows and hens aren't immediately killed in order to produce milk and eggs, the animals suffer terrible and repeated exploitation of their reproductive labor and their male offspring are killed soon after birth. And cows like Norma and Ebony are killed much earlier than they would otherwise die naturally when they become "spent," that is, when they stop producing as much milk. But many utilitarians don't worry about killing at all, if it is done quickly and painlessly.

The idea of painless killing is much more theoretical than many animal ethicists acknowledge. It has very little do with the practice in most small organic so-called "humane" dairies, where cows often suffer acutely. In addition to artificially inseminating cows, removing their calves at birth, and killing the males, small operations by and large slaughter cows in the same way as intensive farming operations, exposing them to the terror of transport to industrial abattoirs where their bodies are callously "processed" on assembly lines. A very few farmers go to great lengths to have the animals they raise more respectfully killed, above all, by scheduling them for slaughter in small mobile slaughter units (MSUs). Yet, despite the fact that MSUs kill many fewer animals, their techniques are similar to those of industrial slaughterhouses: "Animals are stunned with a captive bolt gun (or a firearm), sometimes taking two or three shots to render the animal unconscious. The animal's throat is then slit and the body hung to bleed out, be disemboweled, and dismembered" (Gruen and Jones 2015: 161). It is unsurprising that cows suffer greatly at small dairies given that these farms are part of society-wide practices of treating the reproductive capacities, bodies, and secretions of cows as commodities for exchange. It is arguably irresponsible fantasy to imagine that these institutions could be organized to regard the suffering of the very creatures they commodify as important enough to justify arrangements for painless killing.

Fantasy or not, many utilitarians regularly imagine that there is a real possibility of painlessly killing cows and other animals used for food. Some even imagine we might be able to genetically alter animals so that they die young, after a short and happy life, so no one actually has to get blood on their hands. This idea allows people to eat "animals the nice way," as Jeff McMahan (2008) suggests. People would presumably have pleasure eating animals, and their milk and eggs, and, if they were all raised humanely, it seems like a "win–win."

But one can only think of it as a win for the animals if we reduce contentment to the absence of physical pain, reduce individual cows to containers of contentment, and reject as irrelevant any perception of them as complex individuals with deep social attachments. Not unlike the industry that commodifies their reproductive capacities, utilitarians quantify their pleasant and unpleasant experiences, blotting out the sort of recognition of individual animals that would enable us to respond appropriately to the value of their lives and relationships and to empathize with their readiness to risk their lives to save their young.

A few weeks after Norma and Nina began settling in at VINE, staff found Ebony in the barn in the back pasture with a new-born calf. Because Ebony was so thin when she arrived at the sanctuary, about seven months before the birth of the new calf, and was still nursing Ivory, the fact that she had put on weight wasn't particularly remarkable. In all likelihood, she had a sexual encounter while she was in the woods, with her companion who was killed. When Ebony and her new infant were brought down the hill, they got to meet Norma and Nina. Nina and the new calf Cora are roughly the same age and will grow up together. Norma and Ebony have formed a friendship. Norma was comfortable enough to allow Ebony to keep an eye on Nina while she explored and then Norma returned the favor. Utilitarianism can't help us in thinking about the ethical significance of these aspects of cows' lives. Using theoretical tools that oblige them to treat these animals as replaceable vessels of pleasure and pain, consequentialists take themselves out of the business of registering the importance of their relationships with offspring, of the value of their freedom from exploitation, or of the meaning of their budding friendships.

Equal Consideration

When, in the late twentieth century, animal ethics started to achieve recognition as a legitimate academic field, many of the field's most influential arguments for regarding animals as morally significant beings were formulated in utilitarian terms. Animal ethicists who incline toward utilitarianism often represent themselves as inheriting their concern for animals from philosopher Jeremy Bentham, the founder of modern utilitarianism. At the opening of *Animal Liberation*, Singer credits Bentham with holding that animal suffering and enjoyment are as important morally as human suffering and enjoyment. Singer cites a now oft-cited note at the end of Bentham's 1789 *Introduction to the Principles of Morals and Legislation* in which Bentham anticipates a day at which it is "recognized that the number of the legs, the villosity of the skin, or the termination of the *os sacrum* are reasons . . . insufficient for abandoning a sensitive being [without redress to the caprice of a tormenter]." Bentham continues:

> What else is it that should trace the insuperable line? Is it the faculty of reason, or perhaps the faculty of discourse? But a full-grown horse or dog is beyond comparison a more rational, as well as a more conversable animal, than an infant of a day or a week or even a month, old. But suppose they were otherwise, what would it avail? The question is not, Can they *reason*? nor Can they *talk*? But, Can they *suffer*? (Cited in Singer 2009 [1975]: 7)

Bentham is not as apt a forerunner of utilitarian animal ethics as Singer and others have suggested (see also Ryder 1975). Bentham opposed wanton cruelty to animals, but he held that animal suffering was less significant than human suffering, and he defended not only the slaughter of animals for food but also experimentation that led to the suffering and death of animals (see Boddice 2010: 473–5). Still, he did take the step of placing animals within the sphere of moral considerability in virtue of their capacities to suffer.

Two points are important when discussing the historical role and continuing appeal of utilitarianism within animal ethics. One is that it furnishes an attractively – if also deceptively – simple account of how it is that animals as well as humans matter morally. Or, to make this point with a bit of ethical shop-talk, utilitarianism furnishes an attractively simple account of animal and human "moral status." A second point bearing on the reception of utilitarianism as a pro-animal theory is that – and this will emerge from this book's larger narrative – the modes of reasoning with which it equips animal ethicists and activists are, in significant respects, congenial and unthreatening to major existing social institutions and political formations within advanced capitalism – institutions and formations that, as we'll discuss, contribute centrally to the violent destruction of animal life.

What unifies all consequentialists is the belief that things count as morally right insofar as they produce the best consequences – that is, the outcomes with the greatest value. This leaves room for consequentialists to be quite flexible about what types of things can be assessed as right (or wrong). In order to get started in the assessment business, consequentialists need theories about what is valuable. It might appear – and consequentialists themselves often encourage this perception – that opting for consequentialism in no way constrains our choice of value theories. But, as we'll see, consequentialists' commitments place significant constraints on what values can be like. What distinguishes utilitarian doctrines, within the larger class of consequentialisms, is the view that what is valuable is "utility" where this is taken to mean happiness or pleasure and the absence of pain or suffering. To make a favorable moral assessment of an action is, for a utilitarian, to say that it produces the most pleasure over pain, all things considered.

Since the promotion of pleasure and the minimization of pain are the things considered valuable for pro-animal utilitarians, determining whether an action is right or wrong requires calculating the impacts of that action on all beings who can experience pleasure and pain. Pro-animal utilitarians move directly from saying that creatures are *sentient* in the sense of being capable of experiencing pleasure and pain to saying that they have moral status and merit moral concern. And there is surely something intuitively appealing about basing moral status on creatures' capacities to suffer. After all, it seems right to say that, other things being equal, it is wrong to inflict suffering not only on human beings but on all beings who can suffer.

In the opening chapter of *Animal Liberation*, Singer adds a wrinkle to his discussion of pains and pleasures, and speaks of human beings and animals as possessing "interests" in virtue of their capacities for enjoyment and suffering (2009 [1975]: 33). He calls for considering the equal interests of all beings, animals as well as humans. In presenting himself as an advocate of "the principle of the equal consideration of interests" (2009 [1975]: 35), Singer sets up two claims he wants to make on behalf of his utilitarian outlook. The first claim provides the structure for the opening passages of *Animal Liberation*. Singer contends that his case for better treatment of animals is at bottom the logical extension of demands for equality that have been central to the women's movement and the civil rights movement, and hence that, if we agree with the goals of these movements, consistency obliges us to accept his pro-animal argument. This gesture of Singer's is rhetorically powerful, given that many of his readers either support feminist and antiracist politics or at least don't want to think of themselves as opposing them. There is, however, good reason to think that Singer misconstrues the meaning and value of equality for feminists and antiracists, and thus distorts their commitments.

Failure to recognize "equal" interests in not suffering is not the primary motivation of many who protest centuries-long physical, political, and psychological violence against Black people, women, Indigenous people, and their communities. These efforts are generally driven by concerns about systematic barriers to constructing fulfilling lives, including those that prevent economic and social mobility and failures to address reparations for intergenerational setbacks. Such concerns are sometimes expressed as outrage at political institutions for not living up to their own ideals of equality. But the kind of equality that is demanded in these cases involves recognition of, and also redress for, the wrongs of structural injustices, injustices that are a function of the very workings of these political institutions. It is not possible to understand what is at stake in demands for equality without insight into the history and function of these injustices and wrongs. The pursuit of "equal consideration of interests," when not shaped by these social and political insights, is bound to reinforce oppressive social structures, since one of the ways these structures work is precisely by making invisible the historically and culturally contextualized sufferings of members of human outgroups.

Singer's account of the role of ideals of equality in reference to feminist and antiracist politics simply ignores this logic. He misunderstands the historically sedimented social and political structures, built on exclusion, that these liberating traditions have critically interrogated, and this leads him to a similarly problematic view of animal liberation.

When Singer talks about his principle of "equal consideration of interests," he is also advancing a second claim on behalf of his utilitarian stance. He emphasizes that he is not calling for equivalent treatment of human beings and animals of other kinds. Anticipating the protests of a critic who takes him to be urging us, absurdly, to treat piglets and human children the same way – say, by sending them all to school to learn to read (see Singer 2009 [1975]: 34) – he tells us that human beings and animals of other kinds typically have distinct interests. His view is not that all should be treated the same but that all creatures' like interests should be given equal weight. That is, all creatures' similar individual interests in experiencing pleasure and avoiding pain should, without regard to considerations of species-membership, receive consideration that is, in his constrained sense, equal. The individual pains and pleasures of all those affected by an action are then added up to determine whether that action is right or wrong.

Moral Hierarchies

Whatever appeal this utilitarian thinking may appear to have, it is untenable. The focus on individual capacities effectively erects noxious moral hierarchies. It results in normative rankings between human beings and animals as well as among animals of different kinds. Individual human beings typically have different and greater interests than animals, and animals of some kinds (say, mammals such as cows) typically have different and greater interests than others (say, cephalopods). Within the utilitarian framework, this amounts to saying not only that human beings with more complex interests typically will get greater consideration than other animals but also that animals of what it might seem appropriate to think of as "higher kinds" merit greater consideration than those of "lower kinds."

There might at first blush seem to be nothing objectionable about such hierarchies. Adopting the principle that we owe greater or lesser solicitude to all creatures in accordance with their individual capacities to suffer may seem sensible. After all, humans in a variety of cultural traditions have been insisting on their superiority to animals for millennia, espousing different versions of the idea of a *scala naturae*. Some pro-animal philosophers have even suggested that the "principle of equal consideration of interests" doesn't place humans high enough above animals (Kagan 2019). Yet, as reasonable as a human–animal moral hierarchy may seem, such hierarchies are pernicious, as we will argue throughout this book.

Singer and likeminded theorists also commit themselves to the intensely controversial idea of a moral hierarchy among humans. They believe that human beings with significant congenital cognitive disabilities – for instance, those who are nonlinguistic and unable to attend to their own self-care – warrant less moral attention than those neurotypical human beings Singer calls "normal" (see, e.g., Singer 2015). The idea of "normalcy" may appear innocent enough in utilitarian discussions, but it simply encodes the socially and historically contingent, and highly questionable, higher moral valuation of individuals with certain cognitive capacities. Those "abnormal" individuals who lack these capacities (sometimes referred to in the literature as "marginal cases" of human beings) are valued less. The difference in moral valuation among individual humans that these thinkers wind up endorsing is presented as an expression of respect for the principle of the "equal consideration of interests." But, for all the talk of equality here, there is a clear departure from classic beliefs about equal human worth.

Singer represents this departure as obligatory in light of the recognition that, in its callous treatment of animals, our society expresses a glaring inconsistency. His argument turns on the idea that some humans with severe cognitive

disabilities have interests equivalent to nonhuman animals
such as dogs, pigs, and chimps. This idea gets attacked
by advocates for the cognitively disabled who maintain
that determinations of interests require critical engagement with the individuals being discussed, and such an
engagement is nowhere to be found in Singer's writing.
Singer's contention is that there is no justification for
extending greater consideration to severely cognitively
disabled humans than we do to animals who, as he sees
it, have equivalent interests (Singer 2009 [1975]: 48; see
also Singer 1994: 159–63; 2010: 322; 2015: 140). His aim
in advancing this claim is to call for better treatment for
animals. Yet he also regularly expresses less moral concern
for cognitively disabled people, writing, for example, that
if "we had to choose to save the life of a normal human
being or an intellectually disabled human being, we would
probably choose to save the life of a normal human being"
(2015: 54).

Singer tries to temper these points by saying that he
doesn't think disabled humans and animals should be
treated cruelly or without compassion, urging that they lead
the best lives they can and that, if they are killed, it be as
quickly and painlessly as possible. He tells us that he favors
a position "that would avoid speciesism [i.e., avoid the vice
of granting greater consideration to the interests of some
humans than to the allegedly like interests of animals] but
would not make the lives of the retarded [*sic*] and senile as
cheap as the lives of pigs and dogs now are" (2009 [1975]:
53). These attempts to address the objections of human
beings with cognitive disabilities and many who care for
them fail. Despite Singer's qualifications, he calls, clearly
and unambiguously, for the repudiation of the ideal of
human moral equality.

It is pretty stunning to watch Singer move – in the space of no more than about 20 pages – from presenting himself as inheriting the ideal of equality in which the women's and civil rights movements are grounded to rejecting this very ideal in favor of differential moral statuses for some humans and for other animals. His interpretation of the ideal is, we saw, idiosyncratically narrow and problematic, but he is not wrong to suggest that it has played an important role in feminist and antiracist political organizations and mobilization. So, when Singer ultimately makes it clear that his talk of equality does not align with appeals to human moral equality, he opens up a rift with feminists and antiracists, many of whom are acutely conscious of ways in which structural oppressions overlap and are committed to a disability rights movement inclusive of the cognitively disabled. The picture of feminism and antiracism on which Singer bases his pro-animal argument does not track the aspirations of many of those doing this work. Far from providing support, reflection on these liberating traditions speaks against Singer's argument for improving the treatment of animals.

The Point of View of the Universe

The criticism of Singer's view of equality is not a criticism of its specifically consequentialist tenets. The criticism applies to any outlook that grounds moral worth in individual capacities shared with those thought to be morally central, a strategy also favored by some animal ethicists working in broadly Kantian ethical traditions. We ought to question any position that adopts problematic moral hierarchies on which individual human or nonhuman creatures who lack what are deemed more valuable capacities are situated below those who have them.

Consequentialists sometimes tell us that they take moral reflection to proceed from the "point of view of the universe" (Singer 2015: 84–5; Lazari-Radek and Singer 2014). They stress that, within consequentialist frameworks, moral reflection is disengaged, involving dispassionate calculations about which actions, or other objects of assessment, will have the best or most value-containing consequences. This commitment to point-of-viewless moral reflection is the source of some of the most fundamental criticisms of consequentialist animal ethicists, even while they often proudly represent their insistence on a god's-eye view as the mark of the radicalism of their moral vision.

What is supposed to be radical is the idea that the moral demands we face to act in ways that produce value anywhere in the world is as great as the demand to produce value in our immediate practical circumstances. In a well-known, human-centered example written before *Animal Liberation*, Singer maintains that the demand we face to address the suffering of a toddler we find drowning in a pond alongside the street we happen to be walking on is no greater than the demand we face to address suffering any place in the world (1972: 231). His point is that, in trying to figure out where to intervene morally, we shouldn't make a judgment based on proximity or give preference to endeavors we care about, or to people or animals we know and love. It is supposed to be morally irrelevant *which* humans or animals are helped by our efforts. This suggests that, from a moral standpoint, it is irrelevant that the human worker injured by the cow Norma made sure that Norma, in particular, made it to sanctuary. What matters is simply that, in our concern with humans and animals, we produce the most value or do the most good (Singer 2015: Ch. 8). That is the utilitarian line of reasoning that drives Singer's work on animal and human ethics.

Today a utilitarianism-inspired injunction to do "the most good" is taken by Singer and many others to speak for programs of large-scale charitable social interventions on behalf of human beings and animals. Sympathizers represent this injunction as free of any questionable philosophical presuppositions, and hence as one that everyone who wants to live an upright life needs to follow. But this stance is morally as well as philosophically problematic (see Crary 2021).

One significant objection charges that this stance wrongly asks us to exhibit indifference to the individual humans and animals around us except insofar as our interactions with them contribute to the production of optimal consequences. To approach others in this way is, as we discussed earlier, to ignore their particular interests and circumstances, taking them to be exchangeable vessels of pleasure and pain. Early in his career, Singer was forthright in urging that humans and animals be treated in this manner. "It's as if," he explained approvingly, "sentient beings are the receptacles of something valuable and it does not matter if a receptacle gets broken, so long as there is another receptacle to which the contents can be transferred without getting any spilt" (1979: 149). Over the years he has vacillated on this, most recently claiming with his co-author, philosopher Katarzyna de Lazari-Radek, that happiness is "valuable precisely because it is good for individuals" and that he doesn't regard sentient individuals as "mere receptacles of pleasure and pain" (Lazari-Radek and Singer 2017). However admirable this sentiment may be, simply expressing it has no effect on the fact that their stance puts them in the position Singer earlier upheld as laudably radical, maintaining that it is morally irrelevant which creatures are helped by our actions, and thereby wrongly treating humans and animals as replaceable receptacles.

This criticism traces shortcomings of consequentialism to its image of moral reflection as disengaged calculation from a god's-eye view. Since the mid-twentieth century, there have been numerous notable attacks on this image. One of the best known is in the work that philosopher Bernard Williams was doing in the 1970s and 1980s. Williams argues that if, in ethics, we try to look at our lives from an Archimedean point, we wind up abstracting from even our most valued relationships and practices in a manner that threatens our integrity, that is, our ability to be true to our own deepest commitments (1973; 1981; 1985: Chs. 2 and 8). When consequentialists respond to Williams's argument, they typically represent him as exhorting us to protect our own attachments and life-projects, even when doing so is inseparable from moral wrongdoing. They argue that this concern for ourselves is inexcusably self-indulgent, and they conclude that we are justified in dismissing attacks on point-of-viewless moral reflection as being without merit (e.g., Singer 2015: 48–9, 85, 102).

This rejoinder fails to capture the force of the most insightful criticisms of consequentialists' point-of-viewless picture of moral thought. It is not uncommon, as we noted, for consequentialists to suggest that their specifically conse-quentialist commitment places no restrictions on how they conceive of values. The most telling objections to this commitment come from thinkers claiming that moral reflection is perspectival, that it is always from a point of view, and that consequentialists' insistence on an abstract morality deprives us of the resources needed to recognize values in the first place. This stance is characteristic of the work of some Kantian moral philosophers, as will emerge in our discussion of Christine Korsgaard's work in Chapter 5, and it is characteristic of the work of members of a prominent group of mid-twentieth-century moral philosophers at Oxford, a group including G.E.M. Anscombe, Philippa Foot, and Iris Murdoch, who are among the most original and staunchest critics of consequentialist theory. These last three thinkers represent values as woven into the fabric of our lives such that we require particular sensitivities in order to discern them. So, to them, point-of-viewless consequentialist images of moral reflection appear morally damaging and philosophically bankrupt.

Sensitivity to Others

At consequentialism's core is the idea that an action is right when it promotes what is abstractly recognizable as the best states of affairs – for instance, as utilitarians see it, the states of affairs that feature more pleasure than pain, all things considered. This idea is undercut by views that treat values as woven into actions, attitudes, and relations, and as discernable only through developed sensibilities. These latter views take seriously the intuitive idea that acting rightly is demonstrating appropriate sensitivity to the particular circumstances before us. This is compatible with saying that right actions sometimes aim at others' wellbeing, or at the reduction of their suffering. In cases in which the benevolent pursuit of others' wellbeing is called for, it makes sense to speak – as consequentialists do – of good states of affairs. But we can't lose sight of the fact that promoting others' pleasure or happiness is "found within morality, forming part of it, not standing outside it as a good state of affairs by which moral action in general is to be judged" (Foot 1985: 205). Right actions can involve acting, when circumstantially appropriate, in ways that aim at ends – such as giving others what they are owed – that can clash with the benevolent end of reducing suffering. Apt sensitivity to situations at times calls for promoting others' wellbeing, and at times it calls for promoting other ends. In cases in which it is right to promote other ends, it makes no sense to protest that, since we haven't promoted wellbeing, we achieve a morally worse result.

Utilitarian projects in animal ethics wrongly represent the end of reducing animal suffering (and increasing animal wellbeing) as a universal measure of right action for animal advocacy, when it is in fact only the standard of some right actions. They arrive at this confused position by errone-ously touting the idea that moral reflection proceeds from a dispassionate standpoint. This step leads them to obscure our need for sensitivity to particular humans and animals in order to discern whether we are in circumstances in which benevolent action is demanded, or whether we are instead in circumstances that demand acting in ways that express not so much benevolence, but ideals such as fair-ness, truthfulness, loyalty, empathy, and understanding. Pro-animal utilitarians thus take themselves out of the business of responsible moral assessment. It's not merely that they disavow the engaged critical resources we need, in cases of individual interactions, to determine whether what is called for is benevolent or some other kind of action. These thinkers reject the kinds of engaged critical resources required for making such determinations with regard to larger-scale, sometimes society-wide, interventions. The counsel of utilitarian and other consequentialist animal ethicists would have us set aside the capacities most needed for social as well as moral appraisal, saddling us instead with calculative tools that distort human and animal lives and relations.

The human–animal and human–human hierarchies promoted by Singer and others are part of the distorting methods of utilitarianism animal ethics. These hierarchies consist in antecedent rankings of creatures' claims to moral attention. Pro-animal utilitarians urge us to be guided by such rankings in our moral and social interventions. No doubt this advice is appealing to many people because it makes doing the right thing seem so straightforward and neat. But allowing ourselves to be guided by antecedent rankings means not attending to the often complicated and messy exigencies of the particular circumstances we confront. It means acting on what are, in the most literal sense, *mere prejudices*. Such conduct is especially lamentable because the relevant prejudices – beliefs in human–animal and human–human hierarchies – are actually destructive of efforts for animal liberation.

A commitment to human–animal as well as to certain human–human hierarchies is – as we discuss further in later chapters – a structural feature of the modes of social and economic organization under advanced capitalism. The growth to which our societies aspire, indexed to profit, is premised on treating animals and other parts of living nature as mere resources, while also devaluing the social contributions of women as well as of Indigenous, colonized, and racialized people who are made to do the work of social reproduction. This means that an interconnected set of normative rankings that, for instance, place humans above animals, cis-men above cis-women, and colonizers above colonized are constitutive features of the form of life that has led us into the ecological crisis that represents an existential threat to humans and animals alike. However well intended, pro-animal philosophies that don't question these hierarchies and the social mechanisms that generate them run the risk of supporting the mechanisms and doing more harm to animals than good. That is the position in which utilitarian animal ethicists find themselves. Their thinking retains rather than contests the engrained, prejudicial idea of a human–animal hierarchy that seems to license the use of animals as resources. They assure us that it's fine to leave in place animal-exploiting institutions as long as we introduce welfarist reforms so that the institutions cause less suffering, and they thus veer toward simply greasing the wheels of the social mechanisms that have already destroyed Holocene stability and that have all life on earth hurtling toward yet greater catastrophe.

The point of this chapter's reflections is not that there is nothing positive to say about the work of Singer and others who developed the utilitarian approaches that, to this day, continue to structure a great deal of work in animal ethics. With *Animal Liberation* and subsequent writings, Singer added to the growing public perception of the reality of animal suffering and to the increasingly widespread belief that human–animal interactions call for urgent ethical attention. These things aren't trivial. But in other respects, Singer's contributions are not only equivocal but damaging. Working within a flawed conception of morality, he wrongly represents his approach to animal liberation as a direct extension of the political efforts of antiracists and feminists. Given the extent to which disregard for animals is interwoven with overlapping modes of human oppression, a workable alliance among liberating traditions that integrates animal protectionism is desperately needed. It's not merely that utilitarianism is of no help here; rather, it distorts our pictures of moral reflection and liberating social thought, interfering with attempts to give animal ethics the critical and social theoretical resources that would make it politically effective. From these negative lessons about the consequentialist contentions that have played such an outsized role in animal ethics, we will now explore more constructive themes necessary for addressing the crisis we are facing.

Figure 4 Octopus, Jervis Bay, Australia. Photo courtesy of
Peter Godfrey-Smith.

4

Minds / Octopuses

In 2010, documentary filmmaker and naturalist Craig Foster, finding himself suffering from professional burn-out and serious associated health problems, decided to try to recover by free-diving in kelp forests off South Africa's Western Cape, where he had swum as a child. On one of his dives he happened across a female common octopus (or *octopus vulgaris*) about the size of a cantaloupe. Gripped by his initial encounter with her, and feeling that he stood to learn something important, he decided to dive to see her every day. These visits are the main subject matter of the 2020 documentary *My Octopus Teacher* (Ehrlich and Reed 2020), for which Foster himself provides a significant portion of the underwater photography and a voiceover.

Foster tells a story about how his affection for an animal prompts him to rethink his and other humans' places in the natural world. With rich images and a lush romantic soundtrack, the film invites us to linger over the striking, and strikingly varying, colors, shapes, and textures of the octopus's body. Throughout, we hear Foster using the language of love – describing himself as "overcome with his feelings for" the octopus and representing himself as cherishing "the . . . physical contact." His account of his moral journey has a structure analogous to that of a traditional human-centered *Bildungsroman*, involving progressively greater understanding of his cephalopodic friend, of her activities and mental capacities, and, in the process, he himself grows.

The first time Foster sees the octopus, it isn't clear to him what he is seeing. He catches sight of a "really strange thing" on the ocean floor that, his camera shows, might be characterized as an odd assortment of shells in the shape of a lumpy basketball. Suddenly the shells fall, revealing an octopus who jets away. At the time of this first encounter, Foster doesn't know how to describe the octopus performance he has just witnessed. Later, he tries to account for his commitment to visiting the octopus daily, explaining that this allows him to perceive "subtle differences" in her behavior and make sense of things otherwise opaque. For example, it equips him to recognize, and bring out visually, that she adapts her strategy for hunting crabs to meet challenges she confronts in hunting a lobster. It also equips him to recognize that, when one day in shallow water she repeatedly waves her arms up into a big shoal of fish, she isn't demonstrating any of her standard predatory behavior – and that she may well be playing.

Toward the end of his time with her, Foster's persistence enables him to make sense of the behavior pattern that initially confounded him. One day he watches as a pyjama shark picks up the octopus's scent, and the octopus tries a series of evasive maneuvers, wrapping herself in kelp, clambering briefly out of the water onto a rock and, ultimately, when capture seems immanent, picking up dozens of shells and folding them all around her vulnerable head. (This footage was also shown in *Blue Planet II*.) What Foster has observed, now twice, is an extraordinary show of behavioral flexibility, and his observations are contributions to the study of octopus minds.

Questions about the mental capacities of octopuses and other cephalopods have received a lot of attention in recent years from philosophers and other researchers interested in the nature of mind. Some of the most perplexing puzzles they grapple with have to do with the relationship between mind and body. The fact that octopuses combine notable intelligence with physical makeups strikingly different from humans and other intelligent land mammals has created heightened excitement about them as beings to study. The physical differences are a function of the 600-million-year breach that separates humans and octopuses from their nearest evolutionary ancestor, a creature no more complex than a small flattened worm (Godfrey-Smith 2016: 5; Montgomery 2015: 1). To recognize octopus intelligence is effectively to register, as philosopher of science and diver Peter Godfrey-Smith puts it, that "evolution built minds twice over" (2016: 9).

Octopuses have large nervous systems with around 500 million neurons, a small fraction of the 100 billion that human beings have, and about the same number as dogs. While their brains are relatively large, taken as a fraction of their body weight, most of their neurons are located outside their brains in their arms (Godfrey-Smith 2016: 50–1; see also Montgomery 2015: 15, 49; Srinivasan 2017). This distinctive distribution of neurons makes the study of what it is like to be an octopus particularly challenging.

This challenge becomes deeper when it is recognized that octopuses behave quite differently in different environments. Coconut octopuses off the coast of Bali behave differently from reef octopuses in the Caribbean, who behave differently from the common octopuses that live in underwater kelp forests, like the one who stars in *My Octopus Teacher*. Many naturalists have made observations of octopuses in the wild, noting their remarkably flexible and ingenious behavior. Wild octopuses' behavioral repertoires are different again from those who are captive. These differences appear in judgments about octopus intelligence. Godfrey-Smith calls his readers' attention to the "mismatch between the results of laboratory experiments on learning and intelligence" and an accumulated body of observations of octopus behavior (2016: 51). While lab experiments show octopuses to be intelligent, if also somewhat slow learners, observations of octopuses in the wild seem to demonstrate more striking ingenuity. Yet, octopuses in captivity have, as the naturalist-author Sy Montgomery reports, also been described as making fantastic escapes (2015: 16–17), playing with pill bottles and other objects (2015: 52–3; Anderson and Mather 1999), and acting in ways that express recognition of, and are reflective of their expectations of, individual human beings (Montgomery 2015: passim; see also Godfrey-Smith 2016: esp. 57).

My Octopus Teacher, with its brilliantly captivating visuals, soundtrack, and storyline, might seem to be ill-conceived for teaching us about octopus minds. One reviewer, Elle Hunt (2020), complains that Foster's "takeaways tend to be emotive rather than scientific," with the result that Foster "sell[s] his subject short." Foster and the film's production team did consult with three scientists who study octopuses, and Hunt lauds this step. She ultimately offers a split verdict: Foster and his colleagues rely on a distracting narrative, but they are nevertheless to be credited with revealing a great deal about octopus life.

But one might have a more positive appraisal of the film. Hunt's mixed assessment depends on a philosophical outlook that seems to place immersive encounters and scientific studies of animal behavior at odds with each other. This is an outlook on which the texture of our lives and world is made up exclusively of physical things and leaves out anything normative or meaningful, including psychologically meaningful behavior, and on which the kind of sensibility required to discern such behavior seems to be necessarily excluded from our cognitive capacities. There are, however, philosophers who argue against this outlook, suggesting that the recognition of the psychologically meaningful behavior of others, and emotionally responding to such recognition, is internal to our cognitive faculties. They invite us to see our relationship to the minds of human and animal others not as a merely intellectual or scientific one, but as one with an ineliminable moral dimension (Cavell 1976; 1979: Parts II and IV; Gaita 2002). The idea is that getting human and animal others clearly in view requires a willingness to step back from attitudes that shape our perception. While these attitudes may be distorting, we need to remain open to ways in which they can also help us see more clearly.

This makes it possible to see the foregrounding of *My Octopus Teacher*'s "love story" (Arnold 2020) as integral to the film's educational aim. Now it appears that we need to adopt an appropriate attitude toward Foster's octopus friend in order to get clearly into view the arresting displays of intelligence that the film reveals. This might involve joining with Foster to get a sense of "the magnificence of her," leaving room for critical discussion about the ways his stance may be inappropriate and need adjustment. The film depends for a positive critical reception on its success in eliciting from viewers the recognition that Foster's sense of wonder illuminates the world of his octopus. But either way, we are left with the filmmakers' compelling idea that the journey of understanding the lives and minds of octopuses is an inescapably moral one.

In animal ethics, inquiry into the minds of other animals is important to scholars who seek to identify certain capacities that animals have and then determine the moral import of that discovery. If an animal is capable of experiencing pain, then actions that cause that being pain should be morally evaluated. If an animal is capable of experiencing the pleasures of freedom, then actions that limit that being's freedom should be morally evaluated. If an animal suffers when removed from her mother, then removing infants who can suffer from the deprivation of their mother's attention and care should be morally evaluated. The general structure of considerations of the link between mindedness and morality starts with what is thought to be a value-neutral investigation into whether an animal has a certain physical or mental capacity, and if that capacity is morally important in the human realm, then it is thought to be morally important in the animal realm. Observational studies determine whether some being is conscious, or can feel pain, or can suffer in various ways, and once that is determined, moral concern can be attached to the existence of that capacity.

There are a host of problems with this structure. A helpful way to approach these matters is by briefly surveying the history of debates on whether other animals have minds. This history is useful to explore not only because it helps to identify some of the difficulty with understanding beings that are quite different from us, but also because it reveals the ways in which investigations in this area cannot be "value-neutral," as value is built into the questions that are asked, the methods that are used to pursue answers to those questions, and the ways that investigators interpret their answers. The values that infuse inquiry may be apparent, or may be more difficult to ascertain, as so many of the things that we think and do require that we overlook certain complicating factors. This isn't to say that investigators "cherry-pick" results, but rather that there is always so much going on around us that we must focus on certain things instead of others to create a coherent perspective. Scientific inquiry is a social process (Longino 1990). Studies that look to determine what qualities of mind another being has depend, whether or not it is acknowledged, on both our subjective experiences of our own minds as well as on our sense of the social and natural environments in which mindedness is made intelligible.

How Animals Lost their Minds

Consider consciousness. Determining just what might be taken to show that an animal has some form of consciousness is the source of great debate. The nature of consciousness has long been contested and questions like "What do we mean by it?", "How can we know whether others have it?", and "Who are those who do have it?" have perplexed philosophers and scientists alike. One significant way of thinking about consciousness is to ask whether – in Thomas Nagel's (1974) famous phrase – there is something it "is like" to be a bat, or an animal of a given kind or whether instead animals of that kind are "just biochemical machines for which all is dark inside" (Godfrey-Smith 2016: 12). Far from being an all-or-nothing capacity, perhaps consciousness can be understood as a product of evolution that may come in more and less sophisticated forms – from "primordial" feelings like thirst and hunger all the way to the possession of an integrated subjective perspective on the world (see Godfrey-Smith 2016: 80–4).

It may well seem obvious that other animals are conscious given the complex behaviors they exhibit in the sea, on land, and in the skies. We live in complex and changing environments, and, in order to successfully navigate these environments and survive, we have to be conscious of what is happening in them. Many scholars have approached questions about whether other animals are experiencing subjects through neurological studies. Both commonsense observations and scientific investigation have led to a general social consensus that other animals are conscious. In 2012, a group of prominent neuroscientists penned "The Cambridge Declaration on Consciousness," outlining advances in neurobiology and neurophysiology that speak strongly for attributing consciousness to nonhuman animals. The Declaration concludes like this:

> The absence of a neocortex does not appear to preclude an organism from experiencing affective states. Convergent evidence indicates that nonhuman animals have the neuroanatomical, neurochemical, and neurophysiological substrates of conscious states along with the capacity to exhibit intentional behaviors. Consequently, the weight of evidence indicates that humans are not unique in possessing the neurological substrates that generate consciousness. Nonhuman animals, including all mammals and birds, and many other creatures, including octopuses, also possess these neurological substrates. (Low et al. 2012)

This identification of many nonhomologous neurophysiological features might well be taken to deepen the puzzle of consciousness. Yet we can't expect neuroscience to settle these matters. The Cambridge Declaration itself expresses a shift in scientific conviction. The neocortex, responsible for what sometimes gets called "the higher-order" brain functions, was once thought essential for conscious mental states. But now neurological substrates – those parts of the nervous system that guide behavior – which are widespread in the natural world, are taken to be able to support consciousness. The simple fact of this change in received scientific belief shows that neurophysiology and neuroanatomy aren't our sole guides to conclusions about animal consciousness. It seems clear that our knowledge about animal minds is at base guided by attention to things that animals do, to animal behavior.

Naturalists have observed animal behavior for centuries, and the work of Charles Darwin (1872) and, particularly, George Romanes (1892) not only elevated discussions of continuities between humans and animals but provided the basis for systematic study of animal minds. By the early twentieth century, the idea that animals could think and feel fell out of favor as behaviorism became a sort of orthodoxy in the study of mind. Behaviorism, in its most extreme form, denied that animals, including humans, have thoughts and feelings that motivate behavior. Behaviorists, looking to make the field of psychology scientifically objective, reduced behaviors to responses to external stimuli, rather than treating them as expressions of thoughts, desires, moods, fears. Scientists under the sway of behaviorism perpetrated some of the most destructive experiments with monkeys and chimpanzees, involving months or sometimes years of sensory and social deprivation, in order to create and study aberrant behavior. Though behaviorism is no longer the dominant ideology in the study of animal minds, it has had a lasting influence on laboratory work with animals.

Behaviorism also initially influenced field studies of animal behavior. After World War II, an area of study that came to be known as "ethology" gained attention through the work of Konrad Lorenz, Niko Tinbergen, and Karl von Frisch, earning them a Nobel Prize in 1973. On the occasion of Lorenz's 60th birthday, Tinbergen wrote "On Aims and Methods of Ethology," describing ethology not as others have, "as the science of imprinting, as the science of innate behaviour," nor as some see it as "the activities of animal lovers," but rather as a scientific method designed to answer the question "Why do these animals behave as they do?" (1963: 411). Although informed by work in laboratories, ethologists were interested in studying animal behavior in the environments where animals live. Tinbergen notes that "this 'return to nature' was a reaction against a tendency prevalent at that time in Psychology to concentrate on phenomena observed in a handful of species which were kept in impoverished environments, to formulate theories claimed to be general, and to proceed deductively by testing these theories experimentally" (1963: 411).

Though the move to again observe animals under more environmentally rich conditions led to important findings and the resistance to generalizing from laboratory studies was prescient, the ethological studies often suffered from the scientistic bias that plagued behaviorism. Tinbergen was not a behaviorist; nonetheless, he and other ethologists continued to object to any claim that could not be explained in merely causal terms. They allowed that there were some mental states that get expressed as behaviors, and theorized that various "instincts" and "drives" can reasonably be thought of as the immediate causes of those behaviors. The ethological theory they proposed was that animals are born with innate plans that perhaps eventually can be fully understood neurologically. Animal behavior isn't simply a response to stimuli or a product of learning/training, but the result of instincts that are programmed within the nervous system and "when activated" are expressed in a "fixed action pattern" (Thorpe 1950, cited in Griffiths 2004).

But appeals to instinct only go so far in explaining great diversity of behavior. The seemingly reciprocal attention and affection that Foster had with his octopus teacher don't lend themselves to instinct-based explanation given that other octopuses didn't always engage with him in the same way. Godfrey-Smith has commented that, though he has spent a great deal of time diving with octopuses, none has responded to him with such affection, although many do with his diving companion. This variability among individual members of the same species reveals the lack of explanatory power of ethology and is one of the reasons that "cognitive ethology" was developed in the 1970s. This area of study, often thought to have begun with the work of Harvard zoologist Donald Griffin (1976, 2001), whose early research helped us understand what it is like to be a bat by identifying their capacities for echolocation, does not shy away from exploring and naming subjective mental states in animals – their fears, their pleasures, their coordinated activities, their play behavior, including deception, etc. As philosopher Dale Jamieson and biologist Marc Bekoff note: "The adoption of cognitive and affective vocabularies by ethologists opens up a range of explanations, predictions, and generalizations that would not otherwise be available. As long as there are animals to behave and humans to wonder why, cognitive interpretations and explanations will be offered" (1992: 120).

Mirror, Mirror

Being aware of the environment one is in, and grabbing hold of things in that environment, as the octopus does with Foster, or otherwise engaging, playing, avoiding, seeking, or fleeing things in one's environment, are all behavioral expressions of consciousness. Being aware of one's inner environment, that is, being conscious of one's self and one's own hunger, fear, delight, etc., is a distinct quality of mind that speaks to the question of what it is like to be someone. An awareness of one's thoughts and feelings, one's own subjective states, is often referred to as self-consciousness. A self-conscious being has a particular sort of consciousness as well as a sense of self. Are there other animals who are self-conscious and, if so, how would we know?

Many behavioral studies of other animals are accepted as demonstrating that animals of particular kinds are conscious, a conclusion supported by the Cambridge Declaration with reference to neuroscientific findings. Can behavior reveal whether animals are self-conscious? A small cottage industry has grown up to try to answer this question by subjecting animals to the mirror self-recognition test. Originated in 1970 by psychologist Gordon Gallop, the test places a colored mark on the bodies of animals while they are under sedation, and, when they recover, they are placed in front of a mirror. Generally, the animals are exposed to the mirror in advance of being marked so that they might learn to recognize what they look like. Once they have a mark that can be seen in their reflection, but that cannot otherwise be smelled or felt, if the animals react to the reflection by engaging in self-directed behavior when looking in the mirror, they are thought to be self-aware. Gallop's first experiments were done with singly-housed chimpanzees, a captive condition that is no longer tolerated for highly social animals like chimpanzees. The chimpanzees were placed in front of a mirror with a mark on their brows, which they explored with their fingers – poking, rubbing, wiping, and then sometimes smelling their fingers, indicating that they knew it was their face they saw in the mirror. This led Gallop to conclude they were self-conscious. Monkeys he studied – stump-tailed, rhesus, and cynomolgus macaques – did not respond to themselves with marks, but rather persisted in viewing their reflections as social threats. They weren't aware of themselves in the mirror.

Since those early studies, mirror self-recognition tests have been conducted on a large number of animals, including other great apes, other types of monkeys, cats, dogs, pigs, elephants, and pandas. Many birds have also been tested, as well as animals that live in the sea, including dolphins, orcas, sea lions, some types of fish, and octopuses. Not many animals have passed the test, but a few have – one single elephant named Happy, who as of this writing lives unhappily alone at the Bronx Zoo, has passed the test; some pigeons and magpies have passed; orangutans have passed; and recently a small fish known as a cleaner wrasse has become the first fish to pass the test.

There has been tremendous interest in which animals have passed the mirror self-recognition test and quite a bit of controversy about what exactly passing or failing the test means in terms of self-consciousness. The fact that a fish appeared to pass has led many to question the significance of the test in the first place. In fact, Alex Jordan, the researcher who conducted the test that showed that this small fish could recognize himself in the mirror, suggests that "either you have to accept that the fish is self-aware, or you have to accept that maybe this test is not testing for that" (quoted in Preston 2018). Many have challenged both the methods and the findings of the mirror test. For some animals, vision is not their primary sensory mode of access to the world, so looking in the mirror isn't going to have much meaning for them. Indeed, rather than being indicative of a type of self-awareness, perhaps the test shows something else, like a libidinal relationship to the image of a body, without much or any sense of self. Others have raised important questions about the relationship between seeing and knowing, and about the extent to which, historically, the role of seeing in self-awareness has been overemphasized, particularly in ways detrimental to humans who don't see.

From Mind to Morality

The disagreement about the significance of the mirror test is unsurprising. Animal behavioral studies, not only those aiming to uncover self-awareness, are beset by conceptual confusion about the relationship between behavior and what the study of behavior can reveal. Many researchers are perplexed by, or in disagreement about, what kind of behavior might establish that an animal has even a very basic form of consciousness – say, the ability to experience pain.

Something we are inclined to take as an expression of pain might, some researchers suggest, after all be a merely reflexive reaction. Various competing interpretations have inspired the development of objectionable experiments to detect true pain behavior. For instance, zebrafish were injected with a chemical thought to cause pain and then were observed to prefer an environment they had not previously favored that contained a painkiller. Similar experiments have been conducted with chickens and crabs, who also turn out to show "pain behavior." Reflecting on these different studies, Godfrey-Smith comments that "you can still doubt that these animals feel anything" (2016: 95). This isn't supposed to be a significant concession. Most present-day philosophers of mind assume that there is a rift between behavior and aspects of mind such that a creature's behavioral displays are conceptually independent of any mental states they express. So, it appears that we are cut off from direct access not only to animal minds, but to other human minds that would enable us to conclude that another is feeling something. The best we can do is assemble neurophysiological and behavioral evidence that makes this conclusion highly probable. Reasoning along these lines, Godfrey-Smith invites us to assess what he sees as the strong but still imperfect case for octopus consciousness, and other researchers take similar routes to comparable assessments of other animals' possession of conscious mental states. Godfrey-Smith notes that "skepticism is always possible, but a case is being made" (2016, 95).

Skepticism about other – animal or human – minds, is based on the idea that the behavior to which we have perceptual access cannot in itself be psychologically meaningful because we can't observe desires, hopes, care, love, or any mental states in animal and human behaviors. This thought is integral to the widespread belief that knowledge of the world is maximally dispassionate, proceeding from a standpoint that is value-neutral, distinct from any sensitivities we might have used to discern values or meanings. The upshot for cognitive ethology seems to be that animals' behaviors need to be regarded as in themselves devoid of normative meaning.

There is good reason to reject this scientistic view that leaves us cut us off from the minds of others. Those opposed to scientism recognize that meaningful human and animal behavior is discernable through developed sensitivities that are integral to our cognitive capacities. Thinking about gaining knowledge of other minds through our cognitive appreciation of them makes room for a convergence between engaged encounters with animals and scientific studies of animal minds. For example, *My Octopus Teacher* makes this kind of contribution to our knowledge of animals' mental capacities, as does ethologist Jane Goodall's well-known work with chimpanzees, which was groundbreaking in so many ways. Goodall not only gave the chimpanzees she was studying names as opposed to numbers, but she also attended to their social and emotional bonds with each other, and even formed such bonds with them herself.

These reflections imply the need to revise familiar accounts of the nature and difficulty of cognitive ethology and of the study of animal minds more generally. Animal behavior is rich with normative significance, and the work researchers do, in immersive settings, to get a feel for the life-forms they are studying contributes to knowledge of animal minds that is not merely "indirect" and so is not haunted by residual skepticism. It's not that this work is easier than is usually assumed or that researchers never either misunderstand what they observe or draw false conclusions. Rather, in studying animal behavior as a route to animal minds, researchers invariably confront, alongside other challenges of their endeavor, difficulties aptly classified as ethical – difficulties of developing an appreciation of the forms of life of the creatures in question.

Clarifying the ethical stakes of studies of animal minds also speaks to the need for a reorientation in animal ethics. Contributions to animal ethics typically start from efforts to show that animals are proper objects of moral consideration in virtue of their individual capacities, often their capacities of mind, their interests, desires, plans, etc. One thing standard accounts have in common is the idea that perceiving an animal before us cannot by itself involve registering their moral worth, and in order to recognize that moral worth we need to recognize some individual capacity they share with humans. Although this idea is generally treated as too obviously correct to be scrutinized or discussed, it is questionable, and reflections about how ethical attitudes permeate studies of animal minds weigh against it. The moral worth of animals is, in a straightforward sense, open to view in their expressions and actions. Far from requiring the grounding that ethicists sometimes try to supply by turning to neurological or ethological studies, animals' moral worth is something we grasp by trying to get a sense of what their lives are like, to achieve a clearsighted view of their behavior and circumstances, and the wants and interests that we can glean from them.

There is no hint of the moral challenges of seeing and understanding particular animals in standard accounts of animal ethics. It's not merely that the common denominator of the most familiar accounts is that moral status is grounded in individual capacities of mind. It also turns out that, for each of the capacities of mind that ethicists have deemed morally significant, human beings typically have that capacity to a greater degree than other animals. The result is that most humans end up valued more than other animals. While this resonates with the many historical ethical traditions that place human beings morally above animals, it is, as we noted in Chapter 3, a matter of mere prejudice that keeps us from properly registering particular creatures and situations, and it represents an intensely problematic anthropocentrism. It follows from the current chapter's line of thought that we have no need for the sorts of theoretical machinations that lead many animal ethicists to accept suspect human–animal moral hierarchies. To the contrary, moral assessment ought to be led not by antecedent theoretical commitments about, say, the moral weight of different capacities of mind, but by responsive attention to the lives and relationships of animals – the sort of attention that Foster models for us with his octopus teacher, that Jane Goodall models for us with chimps, and that many other animal researchers, animal defenders, and animal activists model in their relationships with our fellow creatures.

It is wrong to build into ethical theories bias against animals who lack certain mental capacities valued in human beings, and it is likewise wrong to build into ethical theories bias against human beings who lack such mental capacities. Overcoming these and related forms of bias is part of the raison d'être of ethical reflection. Although we live in social worlds distorted by structures of domination, in which our abilities of ethical perception are often substantially compromised, a core goal of ethics is to equip us to recognize the moral worth – and the dignity – of those humans and animals who are degraded, often in virtue of perceived diminished mental capacities, and made to seem foreign by oppressive systems, or by cultural or ecological distance.

Figure 5 Rescued rat awaiting adoption. Photo courtesy of
Jo-Anne McArthur/We Animals Media.

5

Dignity / Rats

In 2011, researchers published a paper in which they claimed to have shown that rats engaged in empathy-motivated behavior toward distressed companions (Bartal et al. 2011). In the study, one rat is placed in a small, clear tube that the other rat can open with a little effort. It took a while for the free rats to figure out how to liberate the trapped rats, but once they did, they opened the door for the trapped rats with remarkable consistency. The free rats even chose to open the door for the trapped rats in preference to eating chocolate. In a modified experiment, free rats who had already learned how to open tube doors were presented with two clear tubes, one that contained five chocolate chips and another that contained a trapped mate. Rather than always opening the tube with chocolate and eating it all, half the time the free rats would release the trapped rat and then open the chocolate tube and share the treats. As one of the researchers, Peggy Mason, remarked, "essentially helping their cage mate is on a par with chocolate. He can hog the entire chocolate stash if he wanted to, and he does not. We were shocked" (quoted in Mitchum 2011). The researchers concluded that the rats were, arguably, motivated by what they called "the rodent homolog of empathy" and this is what drove them to engage in the pro-social behavior (Bartal et al. 2011).

The desire to help a conspecific instead of eating chocolate was also attributed to rats in Japan. In a study published in 2015, researchers reported on a set of experiments in which rats were soaked and trapped in areas containing different amounts of water and the free rat could choose whether to open the door for the wet rat, allowing her into the safe, dry space, or open a different door, behind which was chocolate. Researchers determined that rats did not like getting soaked because those that experienced the wet condition always quickly opened the door for the rat in the wet area. Because the rats chose to help their distressed cage mate before getting chocolate, the study concluded that rats can behave pro-socially and that helper rats may be motivated by empathy-like feelings toward their distressed cage mate (Sato et al. 2015).

Back in 1959, researchers questioned whether rats felt "sympathy" for other rats. In that experiment, rats were taught to press levers for food and were then exposed to shocks to learn what that felt like; this is called "fear conditioning." They then were faced with a choice of pressing a lever that would shock another rat to get food; those that had experienced the shock did not push the lever (Church 1959).

For over a century, rats have been used in a range of experiments designed to figure out what sorts of mental capacities they might have. They have been exposed to fearful and painful stimuli, they have been tickled, encouraged to play, exposed to a variety of drugs, alcohol, and other addictive substances (Makowska and Weary 2013). They are the animal subject of choice in psychology experiments. But even though so many rats are used in so much research, in the US the Animal Welfare Act that regulates the use of animals in experiments doesn't classify rats as animals, and specifically excludes them, as well as mice and birds, from protection.

In his dark, jarring novel, *Dr. Rat* (1976), William Kotzwinkle satirically introduces us to a range of experiments through a talking protagonist, a rat gone completely mad: "I comfort my fellow rats where I can. It requires psychological understanding, of course. And having been driven insane, I hold the necessary degree in psychology." Dr. Rat overidentifies with those who experiment on him, his sense of worth is tied to what humans can extract from him. And though he articulates his desire to comfort fellow rats, sympathy and empathy are not Dr. Rat's strong suits. He sides with humans over animals at every opportunity. He is the lone holdout in a global animal rebellion against human cruelty that builds throughout the novel. We learn about the uprising from Dr. Rat's exuberant accounts of his own killing of "rebel" animals in the lab he lives in, as well as from snippets from human broadcasts. For example, this from the "CBS Control Center for the Animal Crisis. The latest reports continue to confirm the global proportion of the crisis . . . the animals have gathered in tremendous groups on every continent" committed to ending their subjugation. The animals ultimately lose the battle, "no scurrying little feet in the grass. No softly sliding feline shadows. Not a single meow, not a chirp, not a solitary bark in the whole of creation. You can feel the emptiness out there." Dr. Rat is the only animal who remains. Ironically, throughout the novel, Dr. Rat proclaims that "death is freedom," and, although all the other animals are now free, he doesn't achieve that release.

The number of rats who do meet their death at human hands extends far beyond the laboratory. Thought of as harbingers of disease and plagues, at least before more recent pandemics, which have led many people to associate zoonotic disease with animals who are eaten, rats have been treated primarily as pests. Pests are a complicated category of beings. Pests are unwanted, they are in the wrong place at the wrong time, but they also are symbols of physical, psychological, and moral decay that must be disposed of. According to Jonathan Burt, "the impetus to understand the rat is driven by the desire to control or eradicate it" (2005a: 48). These efforts of "pest control" are costly, and those engaged in it often see themselves as righteous, oddly reminiscent of Dr. Rat. One recent example of human triumph over the pests came in July 2017 when New York City mayor Bill de Blasio committed $32 million to a "rat reduction plan" to help rid areas that have the most "dirty, disgusting" rats. The various agencies involved in the initiative heartily congratulated themselves on these "heroic" efforts, even before any rats were exterminated.

One of the questionable impulses behind "pest control" is the belief that there is something disgusting, filthy, and contagious about the target animals that warrant full-out assaults on their very existence. The drive to rid animals who eat food supplies, leave droppings, or spread disease from human spaces for living, work, public recreation, and public assembly is understandable, especially so when human beings are forced into close contact with pests by oppressive social structures, which add devastating social stigma to very real threats the animals pose to human wellbeing. But it is possible to sympathize with the drive to exterminate or eradicate rats and other pests, while also being aware that they are creatures thrown into their situations, and that they resemble many of the humans obliged to dwell in close proximity to them in being "victims of circumstances" (see Bluefarb 1972: 136–7, cited in Bennett 2020: 45). This awareness opens up a space for taking seriously the moral significance of animals like rats and other perceived pests.

Many animal advocates, grappling with the question of the moral significance of rats and other animals thought to be outside the sphere of moral concern, defend theories of moral status grounded on individual capacities such as the ability to experience suffering and enjoyment. But as we've been arguing, this stance is problematic in numerous ways, among other things because it takes for granted a wrongly neutral conception of how animals enter moral thought. The stance brings with it not only problematic suggestions of human–animal normative rankings that are, at bottom, mere prejudices, but also problematic and equally prejudicial suggestions of moral hierarchies among human beings – hierarchies that create obstacles to politically meaningful alliances between the animal protectionist movement and social movements dedicated to human liberation organized around ideals of human moral equality. One way to more deeply understand these interrelated lines of criticism is through discussions of "animal dignity." These discussions underline ways in which standard approaches to animal moral status distort normative demands that animals make on human beings, and point in the direction of a politically and philosophically more satisfactory approach.

Violations of Animal Dignity

Not every wrong we do to animals is acknowledged by the animals themselves. Human beings sometimes treat animals wrongly in doing things to them that don't obstruct the exercise of any of the animals' capacities and don't interfere with any of their activities. This was true of staff members at the Moscow Circus who dressed a bear in a frilly pastel apron and made her walk around on her hind legs pushing a baby carriage. Making the bear an object of mockery was a form of disrespect over and above the wrong done to her by holding her captive and making her perform, however unaware the bear herself was of the mockery (see Cataldi 2002; Gruen 2014: 231; 2021: 152–2). Similarly reprehensible was the conduct of researchers at the University of Pennsylvania Head Injury Laboratory, who ridicule baboons on whom they had inflicted grievous head trauma, as seen in a video the researchers themselves filmed. Subjecting the baboons to ridicule represented an additional type of disrespect, beyond the great physical harms they were made to suffer, a further wrong not diminished or qualified by the fact that the baboons weren't aware that they were being mocked (Diamond 2001: 137). Returning to rats: while in some circumstances we may be justified in removing them from human spaces, we additionally wrong them when we depict them as disgusting beings whose alleged foulness licenses their extermination.

These forms of disrespect are not limited to particular sites of degradation or humiliation of animals. They are also built into larger structures and institutions that are central to the oppression of animals in advanced industrial societies. It is now standard practice within "poultry-processing plants" to "live hang" chickens, fastening them by their legs so that they hang upside down before being shocked pre-slaughter. As political theorist Dinesh Wadiwel writes:

> The "live hang" is far from a painless process for chickens; the velocity of the operation makes the potential for suffering more extreme. Birds will sustain injuries and pain, and because of the speed of the process, many birds will be incorrectly hung (for example, suspended by one rather than two legs). Some birds will not be stunned in the electrical water bath. As a result, they will then either

experience neck cutting while conscious or, worse (if their necks are not properly cut and they are not killed), will be boiled alive in the scalding tanks. Annie Potts reminds us that in the UK "up to 50 birds an hour are conscious when their throats are cut, and up to 9 in 1,000 birds survive the blade and perish in scalding tanks." Regardless of what sort of death the birds face, the machine rolls smoothly on. (2015: 2)

Treating chickens as mere items on an assembly line, to be managed most efficiently for production, is an insult beyond that of being tormented and killed, even though this is not a concern for the chickens. This point about additional and unregistered insults to chickens processed in slaughterhouses applies to the treatment of other animals in industrial animal agriculture; it applies to the treatment of rats and other animals in laboratories, insofar as the animals are handled as mere tools for investigation, to be employed and dispatched in whatever way contributes most economically to the research program; and, indeed, it applies to the treatment of animals in various settings around the globe.

There is a violation, beyond suffering, that is occurring in these cases, suggesting that animals can be wronged beyond being harmed. One may wonder, what is the basis for such harm-transcending violations? This sort of question assumes that such wrongs must be grounded in some physical or functional feature of the victimized creature that can then guide ethical reflection. But this assumption fails to register that animals enter moral thought as beings who merit specific responses and forms of solicitude, just as humans do. When very old human beings who have lost their capacity to remember and to care for themselves are living in a nursing home, for example, and are denied clothing, are mocked, or otherwise disrespected, there is no need to look for external grounds for the insults to which they are susceptible, whether these take the form of harms or of things beyond harms.

Some thinkers refer to wrongs to animals beyond harms as violations of the *dignity* of animals (see, e.g., Gruen 2021; Loder 2016; Nussbaum 2007). In 1992, the Swiss public voted to include the "dignity of the creature" in the constitution, and in 2008 "animal dignity" was defined in the Swiss Animal Welfare Act to recognize the worth of animals and not only to protect them from unnecessary pain and suffering, but also to prevent them from being humiliated (see Persson et al. 2017). These proposals are helpful prompts for thinking differently about animal ethics.

New Discourses of Dignity

Claims about animal dignity encounter significant resistance particularly because the notion of dignity is classically associated with the idea that human beings are morally superior to animals (see, e.g., Zuolo 2016). It is true that historical and etymological investigations of dignity often point out that "dignity" has been used in an enormous variety of ways (Debes 2009). But this variation is not very important for understanding appeals to dignity in contemporary moral and political discourse. Today, dignity is predominantly treated as a kind of intrinsic value, or unearned merit, that is possessed by all human beings equally, and that reflects human beings' alleged superiority to mere animals. The influence of this understanding of dignity can be traced to Immanuel Kant's striking and important account in his 1785 work, *Groundwork of the Metaphysics of Morals*.

Kant's is the most significant modern treatment of the idea that human beings have a dignity in virtue of capacities of reason that distinguish them from – and place them above – animals. In the *Groundwork*, he develops a conception of dignity that is of undeniable significance for political thought, insofar as it alleges and challenges an overreach of capitalist logics, representing human beings as having a worth that cannot be captured in terms of exchange. Kant announces that, in his envisioned "kingdom of ends," everything "has either a price, or a *dignity*," explaining "that [what] has a price can be replaced with something else, as its *equivalent*; whereas what is elevated above any price and hence allows of no replacement, has a dignity" (2012 [1785]: 46). But, for Kant, it is only human beings whose worth resists capture in economic categories. He believes that our distinctive human capacities of reason make us, among animate life-forms, uniquely capable of moral conduct and that "morality, and humanity in so far as it is capable of morality, is that which alone has dignity [*Würde*]" (2012 [1785]: 47). This view of dignity is, to quote another German philosopher, Theodor Adorno, "directed against animals" (Adorno 1998: 8).

The idea that all human beings equally have a dignity that is a matter of transcendence of the condition of "mere animals" was enormously influential in the middle decades of the twentieth century. One of the drafters of the 1948 Universal Declaration of Human Rights, French Catholic philosopher Jacques Maritain speaks of human "dignity" in reference to the thought that, in virtue of "his intelligence and his will . . . there is in [man] a richer and nobler existence" than in animals who exist "merely physically" (1943: 66; see also pp. 37, 67, 101–2). But this changed to some extent with the rise of the contemporary animal protectionist movement and with the increasing public attention it brought to horrors being inflicted by human beings on other animals. These new trends were accompanied by the emergence of significant attempts, within political theory, to account for human worth and human rights in a manner that, instead of disparaging other animals, acknowledges human animality.

This includes Amartya Sen's and Martha Nussbaum's "capabilities"-based accounts of human rights (Sen 2005; Nussbaum 2007), which aim to capture the content of these rights by listing, in an inventory of human capabilities, behaviors and activities we need and should be entitled to pursue in order to flourish. It is an approach, Nussbaum explains, that can easily be extended, through reflection on how significant human capabilities largely overlap with those of other animals, to address what is owed to nonhuman animals. Judith Butler's (2006) elaboration of human rights in terms of "precarious life" also avoids any suggestion of human supremacism, treating a recognition of what is owed to others as coming through an ethically charged apprehension of precariousness, a strategy which, Butler notes, opens the door to moral and political community with animals.

These projects are part of a trend in political thought away from the idea that human significance is a function of being above or beyond "mere animal" life. Nonetheless, this idea remains potent, and, since the early 2000s, it has experienced a resurgence.

This is apparent in the reawakened interest in theories of dignity that return to Kant and his animal-subjecting view. Twenty years ago, political theorist George Kateb defended a Kant-inspired argument to the effect that the human life-form is unique in partially breaking with nature, and that all human beings are therefore superior to and have "higher dignity than all other species" (Kateb 2011: 5). Since then, other theorists have taken up Kantian notions of equal human dignity as pivotal for political thought, like Kateb's, on which it is a function of what is seen as human superiority to "mere animals." Legal and political philosopher Jeremy Waldron builds into his egalitarian vision an idea of differences in the moral importance and moral considerability of human beings and animals, as well as an idea of "a distinctive dignity in which animals do not share" (2012: 67; see also 2017: Ch. 1); political philosopher Michael Rosen maintains that humans possess inherent value that places them above animals and "is expressed by behavior that marks the distinction between [them] and animals" (2012: 159).

Political philosopher and animal advocate Will Kymlicka has dubbed this return to theories of dignity that place human beings above animals "the new dignitarianism" (2018). As Kymlicka observes, the trend represents something of a puzzle given the animal crisis and environmental predicament. How is it that, at a time when the horror of human cruelty and callousness toward other animals has become dramatically more visible, at a time when we are facing climate catastrophe, we are unable to properly register that we ourselves are vulnerable animals, dependent for survival on the health of our common earthly home? How is it that at such a time it seems appropriate to so many to theorize our moral worth in "human supremacist" terms?

Hatred of Animals, Oppression of Human Beings

A good answer to these questions must recognize that the denigration of animals is foundational within advanced capitalist societies. It's not that the idea that human beings are superior to animals is a capitalist innovation. Normative distinctions between humans and other animals certainly predate capitalism. Yet the fungibility of animals, together with others deemed animal-like, is at the core of capitalist logics.

Bringing this structure into focus has been a central goal of some theorists in the traditions of ecofeminism and ecological Marxism. These theorists invite us to see that the growth of socioeconomic systems organized by markets have notable preconditions. They depend for their growth on treating the reproductive labor of women and the subsistence and care work of marginalized people the world over, as well as animals and the nonhuman natural environment, as "free resources" (see Foster 2000; Martinez-Alier 2002; Bennholdt-Thomsen and Mies 2000; Salleh 1997). Skeptics about these claims sometimes point to efforts to internalize care and subsistence work, and to assimilate aspects of the natural environment into capitalist markets, so that the values they represent are in a sense counted. But caring relationships and the lives of animals have values that can't be captured in terms of the logic of exchange. The result is that attempts to incorporate them wind up resituating, without overcoming, the oppression of human beings and the devastation of animals and the natural world. Within advanced capitalism, with its structural emphasis on production and its global reach, attitudes toward animals as morally unimportant, disposable objects to be used as resources – attitudes connected to similarly disparaging and callous attitudes to groups of vulnerable humans – are constitutionally unacknowledged conditions of how society reproduces itself.

This denigration of animals is often deployed in quite specific ways to devalue certain humans. The tactic is, sadly, as familiar as rats in sewers. Dehumanizing rhetoric and practices link "unwanted" humans to rats and other hated animals, laying the groundwork for atrocities. The Nazis explicitly labeled Jews rats, and, as David Livingstone Smith has written:

> Hitler and his followers were convinced that the Jewish people posed a deadly threat to all that was noble in humanity ... Both the death camps (the gas chambers of which were modeled on delousing chambers) and the Einsatzgruppen (paramilitary death squads that roamed across Eastern Europe followed in the wake of the advancing German army) were responses to what the Nazis perceived to be a lethal pestilence. (Livingstone Smith 2011: 15)

The Germans, Livingstone Smith suggests, set out to do what many ordinary people do: exterminate pests (see also Crary 2019).

Antisemitism is not the only form of racism to be actualized partly through animalizing rhetoric and practice. Theorists such as Joshua Bennett, Bénédicte Boisseron, Claire Jean Kim, and Aph and Syl Ko write powerfully about what Bennett calls "the ongoing entanglement of blackness and animality" (2020: 5), describing devastating dehumanization through animalization of Black human beings that was partly constitutive of chattel slavery in the US and that, despite undergoing changes over generations, remain internal to structures of anti-Black racist oppression today.

Other oppressions, intertwined with racist ones, are also enacted by demeaning comparisons to animals. Generations of ecofeminists have described how suggestions of greater proximity to animals, and to nature generally, frequently figure in the social subjection of women. Disability theorists have brought visibility to the animalization of human beings with physical and cognitive disabilities, and activists have demonstrated that degradation through comparisons to animals is also one form taken by the denigration and sometimes violent marginalization of the poor and the extremely old as well as of trans, nonbinary, and gender queer human beings.

With groups of humans commonly oppressed through comparisons to animals, themselves conceived as fungible objects, it is not surprising that human-oriented liberation movements often aim at establishing that human beings are distinct from, and have precedence over, animals. Kymlicka tells us that "many people assume that the best way to combat dehumanization is to re-inscribe a sharp hierarchy between humans and animals, and emphasize that the good of a human life is radically discontinuous with and superior to that of animals" (2018: 773). Kim (2011) describes how this kind of re-inscription of a human–animal hierarchy, which she calls the "sanctification of species difference," was a core tactic of the African American civil rights movement. And in a similar context, Syl Ko comments that "the label *animal* was one of the most destructive ever applied to us" and that it's accordingly "no wonder that one way we have historically sought and continue to seek social visibility is by asserting our 'humanity'" (Ko and Ko 2017: 554).

Against this backdrop, it's not difficult to understand how insistence on Kant-inspired conceptions of dignity that elevate humans at the cost of animals can seem important and relevant. This "new dignitarianism" may appear to be the political philosophy needed to combat the horrific dehumanization of groups of vulnerable human beings. Waldron, himself a "new dignitarian," credits Rosen with showing that an animal-subjecting conception of human dignity is necessary if we are to resist antisemitism, given "the pervasive and insistent denigration of [Jews] as animals and their treatment as animals, in being bundled into cattle cars and so on" (Waldron 2013: 561).

Animal-subjugating conceptions of dignity, however helpful they at first seem, are not unproblematic for human liberation. These conceptions are often presented as appealing expressions of human moral equality and they owe their emancipatory promise to their egalitarian credentials. But it is not even clear that they have such credentials. The theorists who count as new dignitarians resemble advocates of standard accounts of moral status in seeking to ground human dignity in individual capacities, and they typically specify that the capacities that are relevant are those like "reason, moral agency, personal autonomy, and the capacity to love" (Waldron 2017: 216). It is true that these theorists of dignity openly contest the claims of thinkers like Singer who hold that this basic approach to moral worth leads to the disenfranchisement of human beings with profound cognitive disabilities. But the dignity theorists are hard pressed to explain how it is possible for them to be wholly inclusive. Even Waldron, who takes seriously the claims to equality of humans with profound intellectual impairments, regards these humans as "hard and heartbreaking cases" (2017: 216), and he maintains that reflection on these cases shows that we need to extend the notion of dignity from core instances, a stance he knows will be impugned by disability advocates as "patronizing" and harmful (2017: 253).

Even if new dignitarians were entitled to drape themselves in egalitarian colors, which is by no means clear, their representations of animals as below human beings work against projects of human liberation. Social psychologists have, since the early 2010s, adduced evidence of a causal link between thought and conduct that situate animals normatively below human beings and the dehumanization of outgroups. There is an emerging consensus on what is called the "interspecies model of prejudice," that is, the idea that "beliefs in a human–animal divide set the foundation for outgroup dehumanization" (Costello and Hodson 2014: 178; see also Dhont et al. 2016). This by itself suggests that strategies for human liberation that reassert the subjection of animals will be to some extent self-undermining.

As we've discussed, the tendency to treat animals and the rest of nature as nothing more than exploitable resources is built into the workings of late capitalist societies. Efforts at human liberation that insist on continuing to debase animals risk being counterproductive because they rehearse the logic according to which any human compared to animals is rightly considered a "free resource" themselves, open to exploitation. If emancipatory strategies reaffirm the subjugation of animals without questioning larger structures that simultaneously hurt socially susceptible human beings as well as animals, there's a danger that, for all our intentions to the contrary, we will contribute to the perpetuation of social arrangements that systematically reproduce the notion that some human beings are disposable.

Rethinking Dignity

New dignitarians conceive the transcendence or surpassing of animality as dignity's mark. This makes the very notion of animal dignity seem oxymoronic. But there is good reason to believe that this approach is ill-suited to advance the causes of egalitarianism and human rights that are new dignitarians' chief concern. These reflections open up space for rethinking dignity in a manner that equips us to make sense of animal cases like the Moscow Circus bear and the baboons at the Penn Head Injury Laboratory, mentioned above. Or consider a case in which dogs are arguably wronged while not being harmed, in which it seems right to say their dignity is violated. In a documentary called *Well Groomed*, about people and dogs who participate in creative grooming competitions, dogs are shown "sculptured with gel, sprinkled in glitter and otherwise primped to Technicolor perfection." Sometimes the dogs are groomed to look like other animals – dinosaurs, lions, ponies, camels, sea horses, and others. Although some people have argued that this isn't good for dogs, organizers of these competitions suggest that the dogs love the attention. But this is arguably beside the point. Even if these dogs have been trained to enjoy this sort of handling, and the noxious odors of the various sprays and gels, we can nonetheless ask whether the dog's dignity is being violated when they are used in this way.

Since Kant is the main modern source for an animality-transcending notion of dignity, it is striking that one of the most widely discussed recent efforts to make room for animal dignity makes use of themes from Kant's ethics. In *Fellow Creatures: Our Obligations to the Other Animals* (2018), Kantian moral philosopher and animal advocate Christine Korsgaard offers what she presents as a friendly amendment to Kant. She rejects his well-known and notorious claim that human beings' duties to animals are limited to those that are – as moral philosophers put it – *indirect*, that is, to duties that are mere reflections of duties that we human beings owe to ourselves and each other. The Kantian idea is that, while we are, say, indirectly obligated not to injure animals owned by other human beings by our direct duty not to injure our fellow humans, there is nothing that we owe directly to animals. Korsgaard's thought is that, in arriving at this view,

Kant misinterprets the significance of his own conception of morality. She argues that, properly understood, Kant's normative commitments support the conclusion that we "are obligated to treat all sentient animals ... as what he calls 'ends-in-themselves'" (2018: xi), where this implies that animals are in Kant's sense elevated above any price and endowed with dignity.

Korsgaard arrives at her pro-animal stance by arguing for a revision of Kant's famous notion of an "end in itself." Those who are ends in themselves should be treated not as mere instruments for advancing others' ends, but in ways respectful of their own ends. She departs from Kant in maintaining that the class of creatures who are ends in themselves encompasses all human beings and nonhuman animals. A cornerstone of Kant's moral philosophy is that a reason is morally acceptable if it involves a principle of action (a "maxim") that would consistently hold up if everyone acted according to it ("universalization"), and Korsgaard adopts this Kantian idea. Kant takes moral action to be legislating moral laws that apply only to ends in themselves, and his official view is that human legislators exhaust the pool of these ends in themselves. Korsgaard criticizes Kant for this human exclusivity. On her revised Kantian view, to say that "a creature is an end in itself" is just to say that "we should accord the creature the kind of value that as a living creature she necessarily accords to herself" (2018: 137). For her, animals are ends in themselves and, as such, bearers of dignity.

Korsgaard's work on animals has been especially well received among philosophers, many of whom find something congenial in her particular neo-Kantian style of ethical theorizing. Korsgaard is admirable for presenting an account of moral thought on which it is perspectival, eschewing any suggestion of point-of-viewlessness, and also universally authoritative. She seems to manage this feat in a way that respects the constraints of an entrenched view of the world on which "natural facts do not by themselves have normative implications" (2018: 95). She demonstrates her respect for this view by treating evaluations of prospective reasons as matters not of getting factual claims about the world right, but of identifying maxims with universalizable forms. The exercise of discerning universalizability, as Korsgaard conceives it, presupposes that all values are, to use her signature term, "tethered" in the sense of being attached to particular creatures' valuing (2018: 9). In asking whether our maxims universalize, we are asking whether, if everyone acted on them, this would be consistent with according nonhuman as well as human creatures the value they accord themselves, and this, significantly, is a question we ask from the standpoint of "empathy" with our fellow creatures (2018: 13–15, 21 and passim). Korsgaard's outlook seems appealing in that it accommodates a widely accepted worldview, while telling a story about universally authoritative moral thought on which it is irreducibly perspectival, instead of the implausible view from nowhere to which consequentialists are wedded, as we discussed in Chapter 3.

For all of these reasons, Korsgaard's strategy for talking about animal dignity may seem attractive. The problem is that it doesn't work. The trouble has to do with the fact that, in talking about maxims, the principles of our actions, we use the kinds of ethically charged categories that, as we saw in Chapter 4, we employ in thinking about our own and others' intentional and expressive behaviors. Korsgaard universalizes because she wants to do ethics without presupposing that the discernment of value comes through attention to the world. When we're trying to universalize maxims that involve ethically loaded concepts, we can only stay clear of this presupposition if we assume that it's possible to disentangle the evaluative and descriptive components of the concepts' meanings. A great deal of ink has been spilled by philosophers who think we must be able to separate the evaluative and descriptive components of the meanings of ethical concepts, and many highly involved strategies have been proposed. But the success of these efforts is questionable. Korsgaard's revised Kantian strategy of universalizing depends on the very value-laden image of the world that it is supposed to enable us to relinquish; the moral heavy lifting in her work is in fact being done not by the kind of universalizability test she foregrounds, but rather by a kind of moral attention to the worldly lives of human beings and animals that she dismisses from the get-go.

This negative lesson about Korsgaard's enterprise contains the seed of a positive lesson about how to make sense of the notion of animal dignity. Korsgaard's neo-Kantian strategy founders because she grounds it in an untenable fact/value divide, a divide that is morally as well as philosophically flawed. Facts aren't free of values, and some values are experientially discernable. Korsgaard's view, and the views of many others in animal ethics, block recognition of the irredeemably ethical dimension of attempts to do empirical justice in ethics to human and nonhuman animals. This recognition is decisive for understanding animal dignity. That is because getting rats and other animals into view is essential for appreciating that they merit respect and solicitude, and that they are directly vulnerable to harms and wrongs. Showing that rats and other animals are bearers of dignity requires, we might say, making their lives visible.

Figure 6 Woodstock and Volan at Foster Parrots Sanctuary in Rhode Island. Photo courtesy of Brian Jones.

6

Seeing / Parrots

Parrots regularly appear in literature as symbolic representations of intimate connections to the natural world. They also act as truth-tellers, even when the secrets they reveal lead to their own deaths. Sometimes, as with the parrot in Gabriel García Márquez's 1985 novel *Love in the Time of Cholera*, the parrot is a stand-in for the author. In an obituary for this late master of magical realism, Kathryn Schulz (2014) asks: "What kind of self-respecting *un*magical world would be home to such magic-marker birds, birds that know how to talk and that live eighty years and more?" "Colorful, extravagant, blasphemous, polyglot, erudite, protective, and mischievous, with an unfathomable mind and an extraordinary voice," the parrot, she suggests, was the author "trapped in another kind of body, as happens sometimes in fairy tales as myths." In a quirky *New York Times* commentary entitled "My Parrot, My Self," Anthony Gottlieb (2008) notes that "at least since the early Middle Ages, fictional parrots have been credited with unnatural wisdom and sometimes even foresight." Because parrots can speak human languages, one needn't be Dr. Dolittle to understand what the animals might be thinking.

In Hugh Lofting's tale (1988 [1920]), Dr. Dolittle had a significant relationship with the parrot Polynesia, even before he talked to the other animals, and she herself had some critical thoughts to share:

One afternoon when the Doctor was busy writing in a book, Polynesia sat in the window – as she nearly always did – looking out at the leaves blowing about in the garden. Presently she laughed aloud.

"What is it, Polynesia?" asked the Doctor, looking up from his book.

"I was just thinking," said the parrot; and she went on looking at the leaves.

"What were you thinking?"

"I was thinking about people," said Polynesia. "People make me sick. They think they're so wonderful. The world has been going on now for thousands of years, hasn't it? And the only thing in animal-language that PEOPLE have learned to understand is that when a dog wags his tail he means 'I'm glad!' – It's funny, isn't it? You are the very first man to talk like us. Oh, sometimes people annoy me dreadfully – such airs they put on – talking about 'the dumb animals.' DUMB! – Huh! … PEOPLE, Golly! I suppose if people ever learn to fly – like any common hedge-sparrow – we shall never hear the end of it!"

Dr. Dolittle was originally published in 1920, so Lofting couldn't know what would befall parrots when humans did "learn to fly" across oceans. Deforestation and habitat destruction have led to threats of extinction to a range of animals, including these birds. The development and expansion of the trade in exotic animals has had a particularly devastating impact on parrots, who have a higher extinction rate today than any other bird group.

There are 398 species of colorful parrots – that includes lorikeets and parakeets, macaws, cockatiels and cockatoos, and the New Zealand kakapo, among others. Of these, 111 species, or 28 percent of the existing bird species, are considered threatened; 17 species are critically endangered; and 56 percent of all parrot species are in decline. Parrots are the most common bird to be subject to the illegal trade in wildlife. According to a 2016 study, of the 16 parrot species that are now extinct, 6 were used as pets. Today, 372 species are used as pets, and that may very well threaten their continued existence in the wild (Olah et al. 2016). After dogs, cats, and fish, parrots are the next most popular pets in the world. The desire to own these beautiful birds has led to a lucrative illegal trade.

Importing exotic pets of all sorts is, worldwide, a massive multibillion-dollar business (Lockwood et al. 2019). Illegal poaching and sales contribute to the threatened status of 66 parrot species. Several laws prohibiting the capture and export of wild-caught birds have slowed, but not ended, the trade in parrots. This includes the Convention on International Trade in Endangered Species (CITES), a 1975 treaty meant to protect wildlife; the 1992 Wild Bird Conservation Act (WBCA) meant to stop the illegal parrot trade in the United States; and the 2007 European Union ban on the importation of all wild birds. The World Wildlife Fund (WWF) estimated that between 1998 and 2000, one million parrots were traded (Gastanaga et al. 2010), and some estimates suggest that up to 75 percent of smuggled parrots die in transport (US Department of Interior 2020). Though the number of parrots traded has since declined, the illegal trafficking continues.

Part of the reason the trade hasn't been stopped is a loophole that smugglers take advantage of – none of the regulations succeeds in prohibiting the captive breeding of parrots. Claiming that parrots and other smuggled species are captive-born provides cover for those engaged in the illegal trade. But not everyone gets away with it. Johann Zillinger spent three decades smuggling animals, and is reported to have obtained valid CITES documents to disguise smuggled animals as captive-bred. He boastfully chastised smugglers of other illegal goods: "Why would anyone traffic drugs or weapons? They're idiots. With wildlife, the profits are much higher, and there's no risk." In 2015, however, Zillinger was caught. "The police knew he was transporting two Lear's macaws . . . As few as 250 of these parrots remain in the wild, leaving the market price up to the highest bidder. Mr. Zillinger bought them for about $8,000 each, but said they would resell for several times that" (Hruby 2020).

Another reason that the trade hasn't stopped is that the countries in which the parrots are native lack the resources to uphold the law and crackdown on illegal trafficking. The lucrative trade provides an income for people who may not have other opportunities. The sale of one scarlet macaw, for example, could fetch enough money for poor and Indigenous people to live for a year. In a 2009 in-depth investigation, Charles Bergman went to Ecuador and traveled with parrot traffickers, then reported on his experiences in the *Smithsonian Magazine*. He recounts the story of a pair of scarlet macaws guarding their nest in a tree in the jungle. One of the native hunters with whom he was traveling said they would cut the tree if there were chicks in the nest, but, if there were eggs, they would have to return to cut the tree later. There were eggs, so they planned to return. Bergman (2009) reports that, on their return:

> When we rounded the bend near the nest, the two macaws were sitting together on a branch . . . Then we saw the fresh footprints on the shore. We raced to the nest. The tree lay on the ground, smashed and wet. There were no chicks. All that remained were a few wet and mangled

feathers near the nest hole . . . We did not know whether the babies survived the crash of the tree onto the ground. (A recent study in Peru found that 48 percent of all blue-and-yellow macaws die when their trees are felled.) Even after the nest had been robbed, the parent macaws had stayed by the downed tree, the image of fidelity and loss.

Rare parrots are desirable to some collectors, precisely because they are rare, but studies have suggested that most people who buy parrots do so because of their beauty, and their attractiveness fetches a higher price. The beautiful green red-lored Amazon parrot population has declined by 80 percent, and the main reason is illegal hunting for the pet trade; "the birds' beauty – and human weakness for colorful creatures – is intrinsic to their downfall" (Lowen 2021). The beautiful blue Spix's macaw, made famous in the animated movie *Rio* (Saldanha 2011), is extinct in the wild due to their popularity as pets. Their beauty hastened the transformation of these gorgeous, wild beings into commodities, but, as it turns out, these long-lived, intelligent birds only do well under social and physical conditions that are almost impossible to establish in a house or aviary, and that makes keeping them as pets truly challenging.

Most parrots pair bond for life. Their attachment to their mates and their offspring is probably what motivates the loyalty the parent macaws showed for their stolen, emptied nest. When parrots are kept as pets, they are often without others of their kind, and they bond deeply with one human. This is so common that those who keep parrots as pets have a name for them: they are referred to as "one-person birds." There are online forums that try to help parrot owners overcome the aggression and other difficulties that develop when the "one-person" parrot becomes intolerant of other members of the human family. Given that parrots live very long lives, between 20 and 80 years, this intense bonding can set off a range of destructive behaviors when the bird's person dies, as no one can replace the deceased individual for that bird.

Parrots can also be loud and opinionated; they bite, chew on furniture, computer and appliance cords, and other household objects, and will pluck out their feathers or injure themselves when denied enough emotional and cognitive stimulation to occupy their complex minds. They are wild animals, even when born in captivity, and many develop psychological problems when kept in cages. Jane Goodall (2011) laments: "For me, the sight of a parrot living alone, living in a cage, deprived of flight, miserably bored, breaks my heart. And the parrot's too, perhaps."

It is estimated that up to 40 million parrots live in captivity in the US, but because they can be so difficult to live with, many parrot owners realize that they can't provide for their beautiful pets. Thousands are surrendered to sanctuaries, where there are long waiting lists. Foster Parrots, a sanctuary in Rhode Island, reports they get at least one call a day from someone who wants to give up their parrot. Parrots who were smuggled into the country from the wild suffer terribly from the trauma of capture, loss of their parents, and transport, and they rarely adjust to their captive lives. But parrots born in captivity suffer as well. Most of the 3–5 million captive parrots born annually in the US are deprived of their mothers and instead are human-reared, a process that undermines their ability to develop parrot behaviors, leaving them psychologically unhealthy. Most of the zoos that hold parrots around the world resist hand-rearing, opting to leave chicks with their parents, except in cases where they would otherwise die, and only then will hand-rearing occur (Parrot Taxon Advisory Group 2016: 34).

Even when a captive parrot is provided with a healthy upbringing with other parrots and is cared for well, they are nonetheless denied their most fundamental freedom, the opportunity to fly. Parrots captive in homes as pets, and exhibited in zoos and aquaria, have their flight restricted. Parrots living in cages may seem uninterested in flying, but this may be a response to frustration. In exhibits, parrots are often kept in aviaries where they may initially fly, but become despondent because their flight is limited, and they experience a type of learned helplessness, which may make them appear uninterested. Even very large aviaries can't support natural flight behavior. Marc Johnson, founder of Foster Parrots, says that "when people ask [him] what is the right-sized cage for a macaw," he can only say "there is no right-sized cage . . . it's thirty-five square miles . . . it's huge, and it's the sky" (from an interview in Argo 2013).

It may be pleasurable for humans to look at beautiful parrots in zoos and aquaria, and many zoos may have acquired their parrots from pet owners who could not find sanctuaries with room to take the parrots in, but when we look at captive parrots, it is difficult to bring into focus who they are – beings with long lives, who usually pair bond for life; beings who are emotionally complex and highly social, who yearn to fly with other parrots, and who would undoubtedly prefer to observe us, if they have to, from afar.

Animal Visibility

That there are obstacles to properly seeing not only parrots but animals of all sorts is a theme of some notable bodies of work. One particularly influential treatment is John Berger's

"Why Look at Animals?" (1980), which focuses on zoos as sites at which animals, paradoxically, go unseen. Berger's remarks about zoos are situated within a story about a social and political transformation, starting in the nineteenth century, and representing a decisive step toward "twenti-eth-century corporate capitalism" (1980: 3) that resulted in expelling animals from daily interactions with human beings. Berger emphasizes human self-alienation, suggest-ing that animals are "an intercession between man and his [animal] origin" (1980: 6) and are uniquely capable of teach-ing us who we are. But this growth of understanding is only available if we attend to animals in a manner responsive to their own look, a feat that has become nearly impossible with industrial methods of production that treat animals as "raw materials," for instance, in the food system where they are "processed like manufactured commodities" (1980: 13). We are heirs of an ideology in which "animals are always the observed" and "the fact that they can observe us has lost all significance" (1980: 16). Animals enter our thinking only as images or abstractions incapable of shedding light on what animal life is like.

Berger explores zoos as the central institutional expres-sion of the social reorganization he bemoans. Zoos display animals in a manner that makes them, and any interaction between them and human visitors, "absolutely marginal" (1980: 24). The result is that "the zoo to which people go to meet animals, to observe them, is, in fact, a monument to the impossibility of such encounters" (1980: 20; see also pp. 26 and 28).

While Berger's account of the invisibility of animals at zoos raises important themes for the topic of seeing animals, it nonetheless misses important aspects of human relations with them. Perhaps most concerning is his tendency to lament a decline in human self-understanding much more than he appears to be bothered by the intensification of horrific violence against animals. But one central highlight of his work, building on a common claim of ideology theory, is that unjust social structures shape practices in ways that interfere with ethical perception and understanding. In arguing that structures internal to capitalist production obstruct our ability to see animals, Berger implies that well-conceived efforts to see animals more clearly will have to go hand in hand with agitation for more just and appropriate social arrangements.

The visibility we are interested in here is a matter of making the lives of animals perceptible and comprehensible. Seeing often involves grasping animals' lives so that an awareness of the richness of their experiences – their pleasures, their sorrows, their longings –is integral to understanding them. Seeing them also involves recognizing the ways that the human social structures they are caught up in are often sites of distortion as well as systematic violence. In these instances, the relevant "seeing" is metaphorical, involving forms of intelligibility that aren't strictly speaking cases of visual perception. Such seeing could also be a matter of hearing the suffering in specific animals' cries or calls, or feeling agitation or distress in their limbs, or sensing a general change in their overall behavior, or observing their movements as they sleep, perhaps dreaming. In yet further cases, the "seeing" in question may be wholly literal, a matter of visually taking in the texture of animals' lives.

Looking at Zoos

During the time since Berger published his critiques, there has been a growing discourse critical of zoos that, unlike

Berger's work, is driven by urgent concerns about the conditions of animals in captivity. The idea that human visitors can't properly see animals in zoos is also a motif of this discourse. What we now think of as zoos began roughly during the mid-eighteenth century, and these early facilities displayed animals for "public amusement and education" (Gruen 2021: 147) and were also sites of scientific investigation. Early zoos were essentially collections of animals in cages, but at the end of the nineteenth century, the exhibits started becoming more "naturalistic." A trader in "exotic" animals, Carl Hagenbeck, developed habitats to display animals without bars, designed to be reminiscent of the animals' wild homes. Hagenbeck's animal expositions specifically aimed to glorify German colonial exploits by showcasing the animal plunder involved. Hagenbeck was also known for displaying humans in zoos (Guy 2021), and he made plans to establish a permanent zoo in Berlin with human as well as animal exhibits. The horrific cruelties and indignities of putting humans on display in zoos is a thing of the not-so-distant past, and zoos devoted to animal exhibits continue to flourish. Contemporary critics argue that the considerations offered to justify zoos' existence are outweighed by harms done to animals.

There is, as philosopher and zoo critic Dale Jamieson puts it, "a moral presumption against taking wild animals out of their native habitats, transporting them great distances and keeping them in alien environments in which their liberty is severely restricted" (1985: 41). It is not merely that this "prevents them from gathering their own food, developing their own social orders and generally behaving in ways that are natural to them" (1985: 41). Just as in the case of parrots, animals die during attempts to capture and transport them, and survivors may be subject to abuse, accidents, new diseases, deformities due to physical conditions, and captivity-related neuroses (see, e.g., Jamieson 1985: 49). Though animals are no longer imported in the high numbers they once were, there are cases in which zoos seek and are granted permission to import wild animals for display, as happened in 2016 when, controversially, 17 African elephants were taken to three US zoos (Seibert 2019).

The idea that the amusement afforded to human visitors by zoos was somehow adequate justification for holding animals captive began to lose favor in the early twentieth century, and today defenses of zoos are generally grounded in their claims to be sites for scientific research and conservation efforts, as well as for educating the public. But zoos, taken together, generate and support surprisingly little scientific research about animals, and their claims to be contributing to the conservation of species are at best highly equivocal, in part because most continue to spend more on publicity and public relations than on conservation attempts and animal care. Importantly, genuine conservation efforts do not require holding animals captive in zoos. With regard to the enterprise of public education, there is good evidence that zoos are by and large failures, their characteristic blend of education and entertainment, or "edutainment" (Lloro 2021), leaving visitors no more knowledgeable about animals than the public at large.

Yet even all of this isn't pointed enough – most zoos actively *mis*educate those who visit them, giving them distorted images of animals. In Jamieson's words: "Zoos teach us a false sense of our place in the natural order. The means of confinement mark a difference between humans and animals. They are there at our pleasure, to be used for our purpose" (1985: 50). Zoos are designed to satisfy human desires, and, whether zoo-goers are consciously aware of it or not, the zoo promotes a feeling of dominant distance for the observer over those being observed. "There is no sense of awe, no veneration of nature . . . teaching disrespect at worst, pity at best. It is little different from watching human prison[ers] in the exercise yard" (Chamberlain and Preece 1993: 205).

Critics of the US prison system have raised similar concerns about "watching human prisoners" during prison tours, echoing animal advocates' concerns about how zoos obscure our view of animals. Prison tours are intrusive in a manner that objectifies; they are "shaped and choreographed to the ends of visitors, and captives are subjected to visitors' constant gaze" even when tending to their most private activities and bodily functions (Montford 2016: 81–2). The worry here is often expressed as one about treating prisoners "as one might treat the occupants of a zoo" (Wacquant 2002: 381, quoted in Montford 2016: 74).

Strikingly, the force of this gesture, as sociologist and criminologist Kelly Struthers Montford notes, is typically to decry the animalization of captive human beings in a manner that affirms the denigration of animals. Those who object to prison tours often proceed by "appealing to the humanity of prisoners" and insisting on "prisoners' difference . . . from nonhuman animals" (Montford 2016: 76). But assertions of species hierarchy tend to undermine the very projects of human liberation they are intended to advance, as we have discussed. Prisoners in the US are not just dehumanized; they are "de-animalized" – denied not only their humanity, but the very conditions that make our lives as animals sensible and livable. As philosopher and prison critic Lisa Guenther writes:

A humanist framework is ultimately inadequate to address the vital concerns of prisoners as living, relational beings.

This relationality can be exploited in innumerable ways, both under the guise of retribution and under the guise of humane reform ... Ultimately, we need a political and ethical phenomenology of constitutive relationality to address the needs and desires of prisoners as human animals, and not as humans rather than animals. The reason why it is degrading to be treated like an animal is because we routinely treat animals in a degrading way in order to dominate and control them. (2013: 128)

Critiques of prison tours remind us how structures of domination and oppression can obscure our view of those oppressed in a wide range of contexts – not only our view of human beings in prisons and other settings in which humans are debased, but also our view of animals in zoos and other institutions in which humans interact with animals in relations of subjection.

Ethics and Politics of Sight

Human violence against animals has exploded so dramatically in scope and intensity that it can without exaggeration be described as a "war against animals" (Wadiwel 2015). As it has grown in ferocity, this assault has been accompanied by social mechanisms that prevent it from being clearly visible. Some of these mechanisms – for instance, the physical, legal, linguistic, and material devices for obscuring or denying what is done to animals in slaughterhouses and laboratories, and as their forest homes are destroyed – serve to hide the onslaught against animals. As is the case with prisons, what is out of sight can easily remain out of mind. Keeping violent, dignity-denying atrocities out of sight allows for a pretense of humane coexistence with each other and animals. So part of the challenge of making the lives of animals visible involves finding ways to illuminate what is hidden.

But efforts at illumination are not always as illuminating, or socially transformative, as anticipated. Timothy Pachirat argues that "even when intended as a tactic of social and political transformation, the act of making the hidden visible may be equally likely to generate other, more effective ways of confining it" (2011: 253). He reminds us of the oft-heard notion that if slaughterhouses had glass walls, everyone would become a vegetarian, and cautions that just making it possible to see atrocious things may not in fact lead to transformation. A political push for visibility may depend for its traction on reactions of repugnance that are partly functions simply of things having been hidden from view, and it may thus paradoxically "feed off the very mechanisms of distance and concealment it seeks to overcome" (2011: 252). Uncovering horrors that human beings visit on animals is not sufficient to ensure forms of "seeing" capable of motivating political action. Erecting glass walls around slaughterhouses won't suffice, just as it hasn't sufficed to have the facts about what is done to animals in factory farms described, as they now have been in numerous books, blogs, newspaper articles, and documentary films, giving them the visibility of common knowledge. The plain details about what is done to animals are important, but by themselves they don't prompt people to intervene to stop the cruelty and violence. We need something more and, as we have been arguing, that would include an appropriate sensitivity to a range of circumstances and attention to the relevant political structures and relations of domination. As Pachirat puts it, we need "a context-sensitive politics of sight [that] recognizes both the possibilities and pitfalls of organized, concerted attempts to make visible what is hidden" (2011: 255).

The strategy of those industrial farms that actively draw attention to their practices, insisting on their claim to "modern" and "humane" credentials, is not to make animals invisible or hidden, but rather to mislead and distract. Something that also happens at zoos, not as mere Berger-style "monuments" to our alienation from our own animality, but as sites for the propagation of a deceptively benign myth about our relation to animals (see Burt 2005b: 212). This suggests another dimension to a "context-sensitive politics of sight" that is capable of getting animals in focus. Such a politics has to involve more than responding to ways unjust social mechanisms occlude ethical perception and understanding. It also has to involve more than recognizing that revelations of previously hidden violence can, when they produce shock without understanding, provide openings for new strategies of concealment. A satisfactory politics of sight must involve grappling with profound paradoxes of invisibility in places like zoos and other tourist attractions in which animals are on display or otherwise *hypervisible*, and in which this coexists with structures that obscure meaningful recognition of their lives, leaving them in conditions of utter social invisibility.

Visual images are valuable for dismantling anti-animal ideologies and bringing animals more properly into view. We recognize this value while also acknowledging the merits of critiques of "mass culture" – or of products of "the culture industry" – as ideologically saturated entertainment that is, at base, a consumable commodity (Adorno 1991; Arendt 1961). The movie *Rio* (Saldanha 2011) is a good case in point. The film uses the plight of Spix macaws and other tropical birds as a backdrop for a pair of feel-good – human and macaw – love stories that sell to the viewer the idea that the world is fundamentally okay and human–bird relations can be righted wholly through individual resourcefulness and good intentions. But influential critiques of mass culture frequently combine attacks on ideological uses of consumable entertainment with affirmations of the possibility of artistic expression capable of orienting us toward the world, including toward those parts of the world inhabited by other animals. It makes sense to distinguish, however loosely, between uses of images that call for consumption and uses of images that aim to open their audience's eyes to aspects of reality. Film theorist and animal advocate Anat Pick (2018) draws such a distinction, describing imagery of the former sort as inviting a "devouring gaze" and imagery of the latter sort as inviting a non-consumptive, world-revealing, "vegan" gaze).

There is a pitfall that it is important to avoid in spelling out what imagery capable of illuminating the world might be like. It might seem as though any such imagery must be maximally transparent, giving viewers, as far as possible, a mere window on the world. An exemplary case pertaining to animals would then be "mainstream wildlife films that go to great lengths to avoid disturbing their animal subjects" (Pick 2015), offering those who watch them an experience akin to directly observing even very elusive animals. But, as Pick (2015) argues, it is fair to ask not only "whether it is appropriate to film animals in this way," but also whether the resulting documentaries in fact promote really seeing animals. By asking us to look upon wild animals as if they are simply there for us to look at – as if, beyond questions about the wrong of disrupting such animals, there were no ethical questions bearing on attempts to access and photograph them in the first place – these images arguably fail to bring the lives of their animal subjects clearly into view, resembling zoos in presenting an image of the animals that is resolutely "out of focus" (Berger 1980). The lesson to draw, as in the case of slaughterhouses with glass walls, is that it is not clear that we approach imagery that helps viewers to see animals' lives and other aspects of the world by aiming at the presumed neutrality of transparency.

Claims to neutrality risk being pernicious because they can bolster even horribly repressive social stances by representing them as "apolitical." Claiming that these views are detached, disinterested, and universal seems to immunize them from criticism. So it is notable that the idea that perceptual experience consists in registering neutral content undergirds traditional ethical theories. It allows for consequentialism's key notion of a "standpoint of the universe" (see Chapter 3), and also seems to explain the availability of the neutral realm of fact, internal to the familiar fact/value divide that underwrites most contributions to Kantian ethics (see Chapter 5). But, as we have been suggesting, this assumption of neutrality is deeply problematic.

Though partly receptive and passive, perception has an ineliminable active dimension, essentially drawing on dispositions that reflect our sense of what is important. Instead of licensing talk of a "standpoint of the universe," an analysis of perceptual experience suggests that it is invariably perspectival and that, in particular cases, we need to develop our sensitivities or modes of appreciation to see clearly.

There is an influential discussion of these issues in the writings of philosopher and novelist Iris Murdoch. One of the great themes of Murdoch's philosophical essays and books is that we need to be willing to critically survey and reshape our own sensibilities in order to bring the world into focus in a manner relevant to ethics (see esp. Murdoch 1970:

16–18). Murdoch acknowledges the danger that our various perspectives and preoccupations will lead us to project ourselves onto what it is we want to perceive, and she warns against the distorting influence of "the fat relentless ego" (see, e.g., 1970: 51). She also stresses that this worry should not keep us from registering that, if we want to see the world clearly, we need urgently to interrogate and develop our attitudes, interests, and empathic capacities. Her work complements discussions of the politics of sight, like this one, which stress that, if we are to advance in our efforts to get the layout of the human and animal world into view, we need to resist oppressive social structures that mold our perspectives in damagingly distorting ways, and to agitate for more liberating forms of life that make room for new perspectives.

World-illuminating – or 'vegan' – imagery does not aim for transparency, but seeks to cultivate the kind of feel for the world required to discern it clearly and justly. Or, as we might also put it, such imagery endeavors to help us develop sensitivities for grasping the significance of how animals – those described by Berger as well as the small cat who, 30 years later, Jacques Derrida (2008) introduced into lectures about human and animal ontology – look back at us. *My Octopus Teacher*, for instance, invites forms of identification with the human protagonist that situate us to imaginatively participate in his stress, relief, wonder, anxiety, love, and grief. It is partly in this way that the film opens our eyes to what octopus life is like. And it is in part by enthralling viewers with images of wild parrots, while also telling stories of the lives of individual captive parrots, that the documentary *Parrot Confidential* (Argo 2013) gets us to perceive these birds well enough to appreciate the magnitude of the harm inflicted on those made to live in cages.

One of the narratives in this film focuses on Basil and Koko, two yellow-naped Amazons, each living with a family in the US. Neither Basil nor Koko meets or spends time with a conspecific during the early years of their lives, encountering another parrot first when Basil's owners go on holiday, leaving him at the home of Koko's owners – and so with Koko. The film shows us Koko when, after spending weeks together with Basil, Basil's owner carries him unceremoniously away in his cage. Koko frantically criss-crosses the side of her own cage, looking toward the hallway where her friend has disappeared, screaming "No! No! No! No! No!"

Films and forms of artistic expression can contribute to our ability to see animals, and other aspects of the world, by developing our feel for what around us is and isn't important. But at any given time and place, societies' concrete practices of interacting with and responding to animals and other human beings embody assessments of importance that, although they may serve to make the lives of animals more visible, may also obstruct any effort to get animals clearly into view. One thing this means is that, as we have seen, society-wide institutions that fail to do justice to the importance of animal lives – such as zoos, industrial animal agriculture, the exotic pet trade, and practices of forest clearing and development – can profoundly interfere with seeing what animals are like. Another thing it means is that the pursuit of animal visibility, together with the pursuit of other forms of social visibility, involves not only reshaping individuals' senses of the importance of the lives of humans and other animals, and sharing those newly developed senses with others, but also acting on these new visions to change the world.

Figure 7 Extinction Rebellion protest, London.
Photo courtesy of Jo-Anne McArthur/We Animals Media.

Politics / Ticks

After walking in the country, particularly in the spring and summer in the Northern hemisphere, hikers are well-advised to check their bodies for ticks. The US Center for Disease Control suggests checking in or around your hair, in and around your ears, under your arms, inside your belly button, around your waist, between your legs and behind your knees. If you find a tick embedded in your body, there is a range of suggestions about how to remove her, only some of which are recommended. Popular myths abound about tick removal, ranging from lighting a match, blowing it out, and placing the hot match head on the tick's body and waiting for the parasite to leave of her own accord, to painting the tick with nail polish. The approved method of removal, however, involves gently grabbing the tick with a tweezers and pulling her out slowly, taking care not to squeeze her, possibly releasing pathogens, or ripping the body off the head, which will remain embedded. After removal, some suggest putting the tick into a plastic bag and popping the bag in the freezer, in case the tick needs to be checked for diseases that could have been passed along. Or you can just flush the animal down the toilet.

Ticks are blood-sucking arachnids that carry a range of diseases that can negatively impact humans and other animals. While there are hundreds of tick species around the world, approximately 60 types can spread diseases. The most common tick-borne diseases include anaplasmosis, babesiosis, and Lyme disease, spread by bites from black-legged ticks; ehrlichiosis, spread by the lone star tick; Rocky Mountain spotted fever, caused by a bite from the brown dog tick. And there is growing evidence that some tick bites cause people to develop potentially fatal allergic reactions after eating meat from mammals. The most immediate indication that one has been infected by tick secretions is a rash, and, once disease has spread, symptoms can range from fever, chills, headache, fatigue, muscle aches, and pains, to arthritis, cranial neuropathy, and nerve or heart damage.

Globally, there has been a startling increase in tick-borne diseases and new diseases are being identified as well. According to two scientists:

> The causes of this global increase in tick-borne diseases are multi-factorial but [include] . . . climate change, land cover change, land use change, population growth, global transportation, global trade, and socio-economic forces have converged to alter the biogeophysical composition of our planet, and these alterations have catalyzed the increase in vector-borne diseases. (Wisely and Glass 2019)

While concerns about the devastating effects of tick-borne diseases are now quite pronounced, and the market for preventative medications available for dogs and cats quite lucrative, diagnoses of and treatments for tick-borne diseases in humans, like Lyme disease, are still rather contentious. Writing on the Harvard Health Blog, Dr. Marcelo Campos notes: "If making a diagnosis can be complex, the controversy about the treatment is so intense that some have even coined the dispute 'Lyme wars.' The clash emerged from doctors' offices, and spread to public hearings in statehouses around the country" (Campos 2018).

As medical professionals involved in the Lyme wars debate how to accurately test for the disease, how many days those diagnosed with Lyme and other tick-borne diseases should take antibiotics, and whether there is such a thing as "post-treatment Lyme disease syndrome," many people suffer terribly from tick-borne illnesses, often for years, even decades. Leslie Feinberg, transgender activist and author of the classic *Stone Butch Blues*, was one of the people who suffered and ultimately died from complications from long-term Lyme disease and multiple tick-borne co-infections. Feinberg, a pioneer for non-binary thinking about gender, using the pronouns "she/zie/hir," describes hir experiences with tick-borne diseases as a war, not about medical standards and protocols, but rather as a war against sick and marginalized people. She/zie described hirself and so many others as "casualties of an undeclared war," which became the title of the blog she/zie wrote to document hir travails until she/zie could write no longer.

Feinberg documents seeing many doctors over the course of almost 40 years, before finally being diagnosed with Lyme and co-infections in 2008. She/zie attributed most of hir difficulties to the prejudice against those who express gender outside binary norms, as well as to longstanding bigotry and testimonial injustice against black people, poor people, queer people, and women. Before dying, Feinberg (2011) wrote:

> I had hoped to write much more about how ruling classes have historically used already existing prejudices to deny the scientific resources and individual aid that epidemics require. I had wanted in particular to write more about institutionalized racism, women's oppression and other

barriers to health care, about the infamous "Tuskegee experiment" and the AIDS epidemic.

I had hoped to write about how denial of medical care for Lyme/+ forces individuals to buy drugs in the illegal, exorbitantly expensive, underground pharmaceutical industry. And I wanted to point out the hypocrisy of denying antibiotic treatment to those who are suffering in this epidemic, while the food industry pumps antibiotics into the food chain for profit.

Although debilitating illness is more common than death from tick bites, another blood-sucking insect, the mosquito, has caused an almost unbelievable number of deaths. In his bestselling, widely reviewed book *The Mosquito: A Human History of Our Deadliest Predator*, Timothy Winegard alerts us to the fact that mosquitos have killed almost half of all humans who have ever been born on the planet – an astonishing 52 billion people. Winegard describes mosquitos as "our apex predator" and "the ultimate agent of historical change" (2019: 11–12). Mosquito-borne diseases include viral encephalitis, dengue, yellow fever, malaria, filariasis, and other diseases that, to this day, kill more than 800,000 people every year. According to Brooke Jarvis, writing in *The New Yorker* in 2019:

> Globalization is helping to spread a new generation of mosquito-borne illnesses once confined to the tropics, such as dengue, perhaps a thousand years old, and chikungunya and Zika . . . climate change is dramatically expanding the ranges in which mosquitoes and the diseases they carry can thrive. One recent study estimated that, within the next fifty years, a billion more people could be exposed to mosquito-borne infections than are today.

One reviewer of Winegard's book argues that there are many ways to describe "our most far-reaching interspecies relationship, but the most compelling metaphor is war" (Bethune 2019).

Mosquitos and ticks inflict grave harms on humans, and humans have been particularly ineffective at fighting back. Our sorry efforts, ranging from mosquito nets to eating more garlic – two questionable methods, unless insecticides are also used (see Yang et al. 2018) – have had relatively small impacts. More wide-scale uses of insecticides in sprays, which can kill mosquitos and ticks, also kill pollinators and many other insects. It may not be helpful to think of ticks, who are simply living their lives, as waging war against human beings. But human efforts to chemically eradicate insects are, in contrast, plainly war-like. The rise of chemical insecticides can, as Rachel Carson recounts in *Silent Spring*, be traced to World War II, when "insects were widely used to test chemicals as agents of death for man," leading to the non-accidental discovery that some "chemicals created in the laboratory were . . . lethal to insects" (1962: 14). The result has been a "chemical war" with "all life caught in its violent crossfire" (1962: 7). The National Wildlife Federation warns against spraying insecticide, arguing that it kills bees and butterflies; that birds can also be harmed by eating bugs who have been sprayed; and that run-off from the toxic chemicals can affect fish and other aquatic creatures (Mizejewski and Weber 2020).

The deadly impacts of these chemicals on other animals is alarming, as bees, butterflies, and other insects are already experiencing a drastic decline. Though insects are all around us – indeed, they may be the animals we are most familiar with – scientists note "downward slides of well-studied bugs, including various kinds of bees, moths, butterflies and beetles . . . A 2014 review in *Science* tried to quantify these declines by synthesizing the findings of existing studies and found that a majority of monitored species were declining, on average by 45 percent" (Jarvis 2018). And a widely cited 2017 German study documented a more than 75 percent loss of biomass of flying insect life in protected areas over 27 years (Hallman et al. 2017). In addition to the impacts of a rapidly changing climate, "insects are dealing with the particular challenges posed by herbicides and pesticides, along with the effects of losing meadows, forests and even weedy patches to the relentless expansion of human spaces" (Jarvis 2018).

We may not be able to prevail in the war we are waging against ticks without high collateral losses of other insects and birds, and animals of other kinds, losses that are tragic in themselves, and that come with grave cost to human health and flourishing. In *Silent Earth* (2021), entomologist Dave Goulson laments the loss "ant by ant, bee by bee, day by day" of the planet's insects, and, while it may be sad for those, like him, who are fascinated by insects, the disappearance of insects would be profoundly devastating for all life on the planet. He echoes Rachel Carson in noting that our war against nature is inevitably a war against ourselves.

The "Political Turn" in Animal Ethics

The conflictual nature of human–animal relationships has recently been taken up in what is being called "the political turn in animal ethics." This phrase was first used in print in 2014 (see Wissenburg and Schlosberg 2014) for a loose body of work aiming to address mainstream animal ethicists' failure "almost entirely to engage with classic issues of political theory" as well as political theorists' failure "almost entirely to engage with animal ethics" (Kymlicka 2017: 175). The phrase caught on, though there is some discussion about whether the novelty of the "turn" is overstated. There is also significant disagreement about what texts and topics it includes, as well as about what sort of politics it calls on us to engage.

Turn-theorists have observed that the rise of contemporary animal ethics, beginning in the late 1970s, has coincided with catastrophic global trends in human–animal interactions – with the expansion of factory farming, the accelerating destruction of animal habitats, and new forms of animal exploitation in research, manufacturing, and entertainment. During this period of increasing attention to animal welfare, "we have made no demonstrable progress toward dismantling the system of animal oppression" (Donaldson and Kymlicka 2011: 2) and "the quantum of animal suffering continues to increase" (Wadiwel 2015: 29–30). Why has ethical reflection had so little traction? Thinkers associated with the political turn answer this question by arguing that standard approaches in animal ethics – those that are "welfarist" in their focus on reducing animal suffering, as well as those that emphasize rights – focus too much on individual action, neglecting political structures and the exercise of state power. Because human domination of animals is embedded in society-wide practices, institutions, and discourses, an ethics that "comes after" these things, leaving them critically untouched, "will merely be complicit in the existing order" (Wadiwel 2015: 56).

Many activists and theorists sound these themes with regard to welfarist strategies in animal protectionism in particular. Policies that ensure a certain level of animal welfare don't help much as long as "the basic premise of moral hierarchy" that allows for the commercial use of animals "goes unchallenged" (Donaldson and Kymlicka 2011: 2). This often occurs when policies that are supposed to regulate institutions that use animals are exploited by those very institutions to justify continuing practices that harm and kill animals. Exploitative industries employ claims about their adherence to welfare standards for promotional purposes regardless of whether the standards are meaningful or are actually complied with. This is a familiar phenomenon in the food industry, where slogans like "grass-fed," "free-range," and "cage-free" figure routinely in advertising pitches for animal parts and products, when the labels don't translate into genuinely improving the lives of animals. The worry, as legal scholar Gary Francione and others argue, is that "ameliorist reforms legitimate, rather than contest, the system of animal enslavement, blunting what might otherwise be a more radical movement" (see Donaldson and Kymlicka 2011: 2).

Theorists associated with the political turn criticize not only standard welfarist approaches in animal ethics, but also standard rights-based ones. Welfarist strategies are problematic because, despite aiming to lessen harms to animals, they fail to challenge the structures of human–animal domination primarily responsible for these harms, and so are at risk of validating and strengthening damaging social mechanisms. Rights-based strategies are problematic, among other reasons, because, while aiming to establish obligations to treat animals better, they don't contest society-wide practices in which a human–animal normative ranking is embedded, and so are in danger of providing support for the hierarchical mechanisms of subordination that make animals vulnerable to harm in the first place.

Noting that existing rights-based strategies focus on negative rights (e.g., the right to be left alone, the right not to be harmed or killed), some turn-theorists warn that, by themselves, such rights promise not to overthrow human supremacist practices, but to delineate mere spheres of inviolability within those practices (see Donaldson and Kymlicka 2011: 4–5). And proposals for positive rights (e.g., the right to be provided with life-promoting goods and protections) for animals are criticized when they fail to challenge human–animal moral hierarchies. Some turn-theorists have worked to remedy limitations of existing approaches by developing systems of positive rights that directly challenge human supremacism (e.g., Donaldson and Kymlicka 2011; Schmitz 2016). This is a plausible general strategy. There is, in Wadiwel's words, "no reason to imagine that rights themselves might not provide a way forward in ending human domination of nonhuman life" (2015: 41). But there's a further set of issues that it is important to consider before embarking on such a project.

Standard approaches in animal ethics can be said to start too late; they fail to go back far enough to contest political structures that enshrine human–animal domination. Yet there is a sense in which some of the very theorists who make this point about standard approaches can likewise be seen to start their own analyses of human–animal relationships too late. Many contributors to the political turn in animal ethics take for granted that any adequate political strategy "must be consistent with our understanding of the political possibilities made available by liberal democracy" (Milligan 2015, 2016; see also Donaldson and Kymlicka 2011: 3; Garner and O'Sullivan 2016). These projects leave unquestioned how contemporary liberal democracies are intertwined with global extractive capitalism. Political interventions on behalf of animals that fail to analyze and interrogate capitalist structures – structures that authorize the devaluation and devastation of animate and inanimate nature – begin the critical process damagingly late. Intervening in these structures is a central theme of some older traditions of thinking about human relationships with animals, including the tradition of ecofeminist social thought.

Ecofeminist Ethics and Politics

Ecofeminism is a political and intellectual movement grounded in the belief that there are conceptual and structural links between the ongoing devastation of nature and the persistent subjugation of women, the poor, colonized, racialized, and other marginalized people. It has at its core the conviction that, to right these wrongs effectively, we must contest them together.

The label "ecofeminism" was first used in the 1970s to recognize connections between the emerging environmental movement and the women's movement (D'Eaubonne 1974). Ecofeminism gives theoretical expression to the practice of activists in many parts of the world, and ecofeminist sensibilities can be observed in the activist efforts of women and workers, as far back as the early decades of the nineteenth century in Britain and elsewhere, simultaneously agitating for their own rights and for better treatment of animals. Inheritors of this tradition work to identify political and economic mechanisms, internal to racial capitalist forms of life, that causally explain the linked disdain for nature and the subjection of women and members of overlapping, often racialized, outgroups. Ecofeminists respond to environmental destruction and interconnected oppressions by calling for a restructuring of our relationships with animals, the rest of nature, and fellow humans that is deeper and more fundamental – and in this respect starts earlier – than projects associated with the political turn in animal ethics.

One strand of ecofeminist thought is dedicated to historical accounts of how, in early modern Europe and its colonies, the advent of capitalist modes of social organization and reproduction goes hand in hand with the use of animals and nature as mere resources and with the denigration of women, Indigenous, and enslaved people. This social transformation is partly discernable in the changing ideas about nature. Ecofeminist historians of science, such as Carolyn Merchant, build on the thought, familiar in accounts of the scientific revolution, that, as industrialization is beginning, "the image of an organic cosmos with a living female earth at its center gives way to a mechanistic world view in which nature was reconstructed as dead and passive, to be dominated and controlled by humans" (1990: xvi). Merchant and others recount how these new ideas are enacted in previously taboo interventions into nature, including more destructive mining practices. Merchant describes how the emerging conception of nature expresses a framework of values aligned "with the directions taken by commercial capitalism" (1980: 193). And she and others tell us that capitalist expansion in turn coincides with a tendency to exalt production, often wrongly representing it as cut off from biological and social reproduction, and a parallel tendency to subjugate women, and especially Indigenous and enslaved people, who are made to do reproductive, care, and subsistence work (see Merchant 1989).

Another strand of ecofeminist thought is dedicated to explaining this centuries-long coincidence of the devastation of nature and the subjection of women in terms of larger political and economic structures. Some ecofeminists ask whether domestic labor and the environment should be conceived as necessary conditions of productive labor on the model of Marx's conception of "primitive accumulation," and so as structurally resistant to incorporation within capitalist economies. The idea of primitive accumulation highlights market societies' dependencies on prior assemblages of goods not produced through market relations. Marx represents such accumulation as an act of great violence, famously declaring, with reference to the forcible seizure of common land, conquest, and enslavement, that capital comes "into the world dripping from head to foot, from every pore, with blood and dirt" (1990 [1867]: 925–6). There is a longstanding debate among Marx scholars and other theorists about whether primitive accumulation is a one-time phenomenon, required only to set the capitalist enterprise in motion, or whether it is instead ongoing.

Drawing on the work of Rosa Luxemburg, who defended the latter view and argued that "capitalism requires an environment of non-capitalist forms of production" (Luxemburg 2003 [1913]: 348), some ecofeminists maintain that the persistence of capitalism depends on the ongoing treatment of both nature and women's domestic labor as freely available resources (see esp. Mies 1986; also Dengler and Strunk 2022). They observe that capitalist societies rely on ongoing expropriation from the earth, Indigenous communities, and animals, as well as on mechanisms for forcibly obliging women to organize their reproductive lives and domestic labor in a manner that supports capitalism's perpetuation. The upshot is that women's social subjection and the destruction of nature can be seen as products of interlocking social mechanisms. "The expropriation of women's reproductive labor is," ecofeminist philosopher Johanna Oksala writes, "structurally analogous to and historically contemporaneous with the extraction of natural resources" (2018: 222).

Ecofeminist claims about how capitalism devastates nature and expropriates women's labor without returning equal value can seem to recommend delivering a clean balance sheet by "internalizing" values previously outside capitalist economies. There are familiar strategies for doing this to inanimate aspects of the environment – for example, carbon trading policies that propose to turn the previously "free" capacity to emit CO_2, and thereby use natural resources as though without "cost," into a commodity that needs to be paid for, creating new markets. But there are serious questions about whether such attempts to internalize nature are economically sound. There are also good reasons, long explored by environmental ethicists, to doubt the legitimacy of reducing these parts of the environment to instrumental or exchange values.

The reasons for skepticism about the legitimacy of this kind of reduction are clear when it comes to the use of animal lives and bodies. We cannot properly pay off human debts for these "costs," and thereby internalize them, because animals are the sorts of beings who are above any price and are not exchangeable or disposable, as we've argued. Respecting animals requires abandoning the notion that they are mere resources and recognizing them as beings with dignity. This point resonates with claims advanced by theorists of the political turn in animal ethics who argue for the introduction of systems of positive rights for animals. But the ecofeminist point goes deeper. Ecofeminists bring into question the models of progress and growth that are central to the functioning of racial capitalist societies and urge us to see the dignity-filled values of human and animal life that are obscured from view by capitalism's logic of exchange.

Capitalist social formations don't themselves provide resources for registering the value of the natural world, including animal lives, and a leading preoccupation of many ecofeminists is developing accounts of social relations that foreground these values. There is an echo here of claims of early members of the Frankfurt School, particularly Max Horkheimer and Theodor Adorno (2002), who identify structural links between horrors visited systematically on human beings and the ruination of nature. They trace these links to the overreach of the kind of exchange-focused, instrumental uses of reason that capitalism foregrounds. Their suggestion is that a meaningful response to the unfolding catastrophe has to involve reconceiving reason so that sensitivities contribute directly to its exercise in bringing the world in view. They are particularly concerned to emphasize that we need to draw on these sensitivities to get human and non-human lives clearly into focus.

Yet a further strand of ecofeminist thought is dedicated to a similar project of reconceiving reason. Many ecofeminists argue that sensitivities internally inform our thought about the world, and speak in this connection of freeing reason from a false opposition to emotion and nature. Ecofeminist theorists are particularly concerned to show that this image of reason equips us to understand and confront difficulties of ideology critique and liberating political thought. They also stress that this critical revisiting of received understandings of reason is not antithetical to reason. "Critiquing the dominant forms of reason which . . . oppose themselves to the sphere of nature does not imply" abandoning reason, ecofeminist philosopher Val Plumwood explains, but only sanctioning its "redefinition or reconstruction in less oppositional and hierarchical ways" (1993: 4). What is at issue is a re-envisioning of reason so that feeling plays an essential role in its use to capture how things are, and so that its tasks involve the sensitive discernment of values. This refashioning provides a crucial tool for animal ethics and politics, as we have illustrated in this book's pages.

The resulting conception of reason gives engaged and empathetic modes of attention a decisive role in uncovering the kinds of values in human and animal lives that capitalist political formations distort. The project of uncovering these values involves listening to the voices of women, marginalized humans, and domestic and subsistence workers, as well as developing ways to listen to animals themselves. We are invited to see that meaningful ecological, pro-animal and feminist political agitation will have to involve, alongside new ecological sensitivities, political and embodied solidarity with those doing reproductive and care work, as well as those trying to subsist even as extinction to their way of life looms. This strain of ecofeminism may be the urgently needed critical theory of our time. *Critical animal theory* is a fitting name for this pressing project.

Untimely Resistance

Extinction not only threatens ways of living for humans and other animals, but "scientists now speak of defaunation: the loss of individuals, the loss of abundance, the loss of a place's absolute animalness" (Jarvis 2018). Ticks, however, seem to be doing quite well in the changing climate. And this isn't particularly surprising now that we have a better understanding of ticks. Jakob von Uexküll, the biologist who developed the concept of the *Umwelt*, allowing us to imagine the various perceptual worlds of other beings, noted the wonder of ticks thwarting time:

To heighten the probability of a prey coming her way, the tick's ability to live long without food must be added.

And this faculty she possesses to an unusual degree. At the Zoological Institute in Rostock, ticks who had been starving for eighteen years have been kept alive. A tick can wait eighteen years. That is something which we humans cannot do. Our time is made up of a series of moments, or briefest time units, within which the world shows no change. For the duration of a moment, the world stands still. Man's moment lasts 1/18 of a second . . . But whatever number we wish to adopt for the tick, the ability to endure a never-changing world for eighteen years is beyond the realm of possibility . . . Only in the tick's world, time, instead of standing still for mere hours, stops for many years at a time, and does not begin to function again until the signal of butyric acid arouses her to renewed activity.

What have we gained by realizing this? Something extremely significant. Time, which frames all happening, seems to us to be the only objectively stable thing in contrast to the colorful change of its contents, and now we see that the subject sways the time of his own world. Instead of saying, as heretofore, that without time, there can be no living subject, we shall now have to say that without a living subject, there can be no time. (1992 [1934]: 326)

While ticks can control their time, we can't. If we were able to stop everything, that would undoubtedly slow the climate crisis and the mass extinctions that are underway. But as planet-destroying human activities continue, we don't have the luxury of waiting to counteract life-threatening industries for 18 years, or even 18 months. We are out of time; resistance is, in significant ways, too late.

This is partly because, as we have argued, meaningful steps need to start earlier than many theorists and activists envision, in order to challenge racial capitalist political formations. It is also partly because the earth-threatening catastrophe we confront has, to a large extent, already happened. The entrenchment of industries of animal "production" and slaughter, large-scale deforestation and the polluting of vast tracts of land and vast bodies of water, and the accumulation over centuries of anthropogenic atmospheric CO_2 that, regardless of possible future cuts in greenhouse gas emissions, won't be fully absorbed for much longer, have all led to the end of the nearly 12,000-year-long stretch of the Holocene. It is at best self-deception to follow those peddling the false optimism of just-in-time "techno-fixes," like forms of stratospheric injection, or the deceptive promise of market-based "solutions" such as the exchange of emissions permissions, projects that strike a chord with many tech entrepreneurs and billionaires, who eagerly fund them, and ruthlessly expand the system of global capitalism implicated in the very ecocide they claim to be averting (see Kolbert 2021).

In saying that calamity is already upon us, we are not counseling apathy. It is both possible and essential to fight the hierarchical structures that critical animal theory criticizes, and that we have discussed throughout this book. These structures not only provide justifications for violent and destructive actions by those in power toward those cast as subordinate, but also block from view the meaningful, valuable lives of these subordinated humans and other animals. They keep the fears, frustrations and friendships, sensibilities and satisfactions, laughter, and the very lives of subjugated beings out of focus, relegated to the background; they are daunting structures and ideologies, and, while identifying and revealing them is certainly important, they need to be undone if there is any chance of a livable future.

Clearsighted resistance to these oppressive systems entails the rejection of investments in hope for liberating possibilities within them. In a shattering analysis of how hope lulls us into a false sense that we can change the system in meaningful ways, Calvin Warren identifies the anti-Black, manipulative use of the "politics of hope" that "recasts despair as possibility, struggle as triumph." He sees this sort of hope as "the object of political fantasy . . . It bundles certain promises about redress, equality, freedom, justice, and progress into a political object that always lies beyond reach" (Warren 2015: 221). Hope becomes a delusive expectation, an attachment to what cannot be achieved. It is a form of what Lauren Berlant (2011) calls "cruel optimism," which "is detrimental because it strengthens the very anti-Black system that would pulverize black being" (Warren 2015: 221). And hope can be destructive in itself. Journalist Michael Scott Moore, who was held captive for 977 days by Somali pirates, suggests that hope "is like heroin to a hostage . . . Hope was a cycle, and after a while, it became a destructive cycle. People say, 'Well, how did you hang onto hope for two years and eight months?' And the fact is: I didn't. I learned to live without hope" (interview with Ari Shapiro, NPR).

Hope, as it is theorized in philosophical circles, often involves an active orientation toward the future. This leads some philosophers who reflect on questions about whether "a life without hope is always (or even sometimes) better than a life with hope to be simply irrelevant for creatures like us." The idea is that, "to live a life devoid of hope is simply not to live a human life; it is not to function – or, tragically, it is to cease to function – as a human being" (McGeer 2004: 101). Yet the very idea that the capacity even for this relatively thin sort of hope is requisite for humanity is problematic since it seems to deny the status of "human" to, for example, individuals with cognitive disabilities who are unable to project themselves into the future. There is also the risk that this capacity to orient toward one's future, when wrongly taken as the mark of humanity, will be given a political interpretation that unjustly denies the status of "human" to many individuals who are compelled to live without more substantive political hope because they face structural conditions that exclude livable futures, perhaps young people confronting adulthoods unlike anything we have known, Black people living in an anti-Black world, incarcerated people serving life sentences, and climate refugees.

Writing about the environmental catastrophes we face, philosopher Michael P. Nelson worries that "the use of hope as a motivator for healing our wounded and warped relationship with the natural world ... will actually stifle, not aid, our resolve" (2016: 130). He calls for a different way of approaching the crisis we have been discussing. Instead of saying "I hope" that some consequence comes about, instead of focusing on outcomes or efficiency, Nelson urges, we should focus on who we want to be in the face of catastrophe and ruin. His proposal is for "individual and collective moral revolution" that involves abandoning hope and propping "ourselves against those forces in the world that are working to bring ruin" (2016: 132).

Such moral revolution should not be conflated with the pursuit of "moral purity." Within the structures of contemporary racial capitalism, there is no meaningful way to have clean hands. Abstaining from the products of industrial animal agriculture – becoming vegan – does not release us from entanglements in the global web of practices in which human beings harm and kill other animals. Many sentient beings are killed within the industrial agricultural production of vegetables, fruits, and grains for human beings, and "animal products are found in or used in the production of a great number of consumer goods"; among other things, this includes:

> Auto upholstery, beer, bread, candles, chewing gum, cosmetics, cranberry juice, deodorants, fertilizers, hairspray, house paint, lipstick, marshmallows, nail polish, plywood, perfume, photographic film, pickles, pillows, red lollipops, rubber, sauerkraut, shaving brushes, shaving cream, soap, soy cheese, sugar, surgical sutures, tennis rackets, transmission fluid, vitamin supplements and wine. (Gruen and Jones 2015: 157)

Although there is no clear way to absent ourselves from lethal institutions that grind up animals, that doesn't mean that we shouldn't do everything we can to try to combat the global ravages of the meat and dairy industries. "Big Meat," as it has been called (Abrell and Stubler, 2021), is "a ravenous machine of exploitation" that, in addition to making workers sick and slaughtering more than a billion land animals globally every year, is bringing the planet to the brink. A 2021 study found that global greenhouse emissions from animal agriculture accounts for nearly 60 percent of all emissions from food production. Raising and killing animals for food, particularly cows, is "far worse for the climate than growing and processing fruits and vegetables for people to eat" (Milman 2021). A co-chair of a working group of the Intergovernmental Panel on Climate Change (IPCC) notes that "it would indeed be beneficial, for both climate and human health [and the animals] if people in many rich countries consumed less meat, and if politics would create appropriate incentives to that effect" (quoted in Schiermeier 2019). And some are calling for much more, not just reforming the system, but banning industrial animal production altogether.

Even if we were able to eliminate the most violent and climate-destroying use of animals, and get rid of industrial animal agriculture, there is no prospect of an utterly peaceable animal kingdom on the earth. Some scientists believe that in the Ediacaran Period organisms lived harmonious lives of little interaction, constituting a sort of Garden of Eden (see Godfrey-Smith 2016: 30–1). Whether or not this is the case, since the Cambrian Period, over 500 million years ago, animals on this planet have been caught up in ecosystems characterized in large part by competition, predation, suffering, and death. Reflection on human beings' embattled relationships with ticks, mosquitos, and other insects, and on the earth system's need for these creatures, reveals some of our own biotic entanglements, making clear that there is, for us, no living without killing.

Yet it is possible, without delusive dreams of moral untaintedness, to seek solidarity in resisting ingrained structures of violence, exploitation, and commodification that threaten the lives and wellbeing of humans and other animals alike. In connection with human-oriented, anticapitalist resistance, political theorist Sue Ferguson (2020) distinguishes two kinds of strategies. There is, first, the creation of revolutionary commons, that is, "alternative, prefigurative spaces like workers' co-ops or communal kitchens." These spaces are, Ferguson stresses, valuable for building new forms of political consciousness, despite the fact that they may have limited reach. The second kind of strategy of resistance relies on "spaces and moments of dis-alienation . . . immanent in everyday capitalist relations" that don't fully disappear but can be locally resisted and subdued. Ferguson is encouraging us to build bridges of solidarity across spaces in which people are already doing this work of dis-alienation, such as "community protests for better housing, workplace strikes, women's strikes ... indigenous land defenses" and youth climate strikes (Ferguson 2020). Her twofold resistance schema, combining the power of revolutionary commons as well as of collectivized revolutionary actions, can be developed so that both strategies feature not only the nonquantifiable, noncommodifiable value of human interactions and relationships but also the nonquantifiable, noncommodifiable value of animal and human–animal interactions and relationships.

When revolutionary commons are inclusively reconceived, some animal sanctuaries appear as exemplary cases. The anticapitalist, ecofeminist, LGBTQ-based VINE Sanctuary provides a safe community for formerly farmed animals, and offers lessons in oppositional, multispecies care. Standing firmly against logics of exploitation and domination, sanctuaries for animals highlight the agency of those who are denied it in prevailing anti-animal systems of power (Blattner et al. 2020). In seeing other animals as distinct beings who are distinctively valuable, sanctuaries can offer a collective refusal of the life-denying social and economic forces that view them as disposable and replaceable. At VINE Sanctuary, animals are encouraged to pursue their own interests and friendships with others, across species, as humans provide food, veterinary care, safety, and companionship. In the face of massive destruction of trillions of land and sea animals around the globe for food annually, it may seem that a sanctuary caring for 500 or 700 or even 1,000 animals can't genuinely be viewed as effective resistance. But the value of sanctuaries lies precisely in refusing quantification metrics for success that prioritize the most cost-effective promotion of abstract notions of animal wellbeing, instead insisting on radical care for particular individuals, beings with distinctive histories, associated vulnerabilities, and unique relationships. And these particular individuals, through their own resistance to systems that treat them as mere disposable commodities, through their relationships of solidarity and support for other animals, and through aid from humans attuned to the value of their lives, collectively model alternative forms of life.

There are other possibilities for revolutionary commons inclusive of animals. Entomologist E.O. Wilson proposes, arrestingly, that we allot half of the earth for wildlife preserves, providing undisturbed space for insects, other animals, and the flora they need to flourish. He argues that we have to increase the roughly 10–15 percent of conservation areas that currently exist around the globe to 50 percent or more if we are to survive. His thought is that we must "find our way as quickly as possible out of the fever swamp of . . . inept philosophical thought through which we still wander" (Wilson 2017: 3). Wilson doesn't work out his scheme in any real detail, and there are straightforward respects in which it is problematic. But his reflections are evocative in that they illustrate challenges of taking seriously the magnitude of the problem, and of imagining a commons that might meet it.

There are also revolutionary actions that clearly reflect appreciation of the nonquantifiable value of animals and human–animal relationships, and some of these are transformative. These include things like attending to those harmed or threatened by disasters directly and indirectly caused by human beings such as oil spills, wars, and extreme weather events; countering the pollution and poisoning of land and water, for example through water-protector actions at Standing Rock; making plant-based foods available in communities with little access to them; working directly to change political structures that govern human interactions with animals and the environment, including efforts to make ecocide a corporate crime under the International Criminal Court; bearing witness in Animal Save Movement protests; and exposing human rights abuses of workers in industrial slaughterhouses.

Animals themselves often engage in forms of revolutionary resistance, on their own behalf as well as on behalf of those they care about. Some of the orangutans in Sumatra and Borneo who refuse to leave their forest homes and fiercely protect their young are propping themselves against life-destroying forces and revolting, as did the orangutan Hope, whose name seems tragically ironic in the present discussion. Something similar can be said about cows like Ebony, who saved herself and her infant Ivory from exploitation, commodification, and death by running from the dairy where she was being used. The resistance of the cow named Norma, who fought when her infant Nina was taken from her, led both of them to VINE Sanctuary where, with solidarity and care from Ebony and other animals, they have been able to live a freer life.

An important component of successful acts of resistance is solidarity among those, animals as well as humans, who are fighting life-destroying structures. Significantly, there is no antecedent guide to such solidarity that could save animal defenders the difficult work of responding to the particular contexts in which overlapping injustices afflict humans and other animals. Interspecies solidarity, an aspect of all of the kinds of revolutionary interventions we have mentioned, is an occasion for improvisation informed by awareness of complex injustices and social mechanisms responsible for generating them.

Resistance of all of these kinds requires forging novel forms of political consciousness, and here there is a decisively important role for the humanities and arts. Philosopher Cora Diamond brings out how prose or verse can evoke the distinctive valuableness and mystery of animals' lives, a point she makes with regard to a poem of Walter de la Mare's called "Ducks" which directs attention to "the particularity of a particular duck, a particular feathered creature, clad in the beauty open to our eyes, dwelling in secret there" (Diamond 2010: 56). Novelist Olga Tokarczuk's book *Drive Your Plow Over the Bones of the Dead* (2018) is narrated by a character who subversively and alluringly enacts her own conception of existence in which humans and other animals act in solidarity against murderous forces of domination and exploitation. Director Bong Joon-Ho's anticapitalist allegory *Okja* (2017) gives its audience a sympathetic view of a fanciful friendship, between a girl and a bio-engineered pig-like creature named Okja, that is simultaneously a rebuke and a threat to the industry that created Okja. Poet Wislawa Szymborska's "Seen from Above" prods us with gentle irony to question our tendency to think "animals die / more shallowly: they aren't deceased, they're dead. / They leave behind, we'd like to think, less feeling and less world / departing, we suppose, from a stage less tragic." Together with activists whose interventions express an appreciation of the unquantifiable value of animal lives – for example, those who erect memorials to or conduct mass public mourning rituals for slaughtered animals – these different types of creative gestures open up needed space for imagining otherwise.

Central to meaningful resistance is the work of care, conceived as establishing and preserving relationships that clearly recognize and respect human and animal dignity, and that contribute to bringing about more just and liberating forms of life. Care-centered strategies of resistance can be pursued at individual as well as political levels. We can create caring communities built on mutual aid, communal space, shared resources, and localized decision-making and a shared desire for mutual thriving (see, e.g., Care Collective 2020). Animals in these caring communities may be active members who can themselves aid the collective. Creating community and caring for those in it can also be conceived as a revolutionary form of self-care. In this spirit, feminist writer Sara Ahmed (2014) tells us that the "work of selfcare is about the creation of community, fragile communities, assembled out of the experiences of being shattered. We reassemble ourselves through the ordinary, everyday, and often painstaking work of looking after ourselves; looking after each other." Similarly, feminist writer and poet Audre Lorde describes self-care as a kind of warfare, since finding ways to exist in a world that wants to destroy or diminish you and your community is a radical act.

When animals are harmed or die or go extinct, the losses echo throughout their own multispecies communities and environments, undoing those of us witnessing their ends, and creating chaos for those in the next generation who will inhabit a very different world, if it is even inhabitable. It is possible that some like mosquitos and ticks and perhaps cockroaches will thrive regardless, but the flourishing and survival of many depends fundamentally on our understanding and disrupting the Animal Crisis.

References

Abrell, Elan, and Niko Stubler. 2021. "Want to Protect Workers, Animals, and the Planet? Ban the Sale of Meat." *Sentient Media*. https://sentientmedia.org/want-to-protect-workers-animals-and-the-planet-ban-meat/.

Adams, Carol. 1990. *The Sexual Politics of Meat: A Feminist-Vegetarian Critical Theory*. New York: Continuum.

Adorno, Theodor. 1998. *Beethoven: The Philosophy of Music*, trans. Edmund Jephcott. Stanford, CA: Stanford University Press.

Adorno, Theodor. 1991. "The Culture Industry Reconsidered." In *The Culture Industry: Selected Essays on Mass Culture*. London: Routledge: 98–106.

Ahmed, Sara. 2014. "Selfcare as Warfare." https://feministkilljoys.com/2014/08/25/selfcare-as-warfare/.

Anderson, Roland C., and Jennifer A. Mather. 1999. "Exploration, Play, and Habituation in Octopuses (*Octopus dofleini*)." *Journal of Comparative Psychology*, 113/3: 333–338.

Andrews, Kristin et al. 2019. *Chimpanzee Rights: The Philosopher's Brief*. Abingdon: Routledge.

Arendt, Hannah. 1961. "The Crisis in Culture: Its Social and Its Political Significance." In *Between Past and Future: Six Essays in Political Thought*. New York: The Viking Press: 197–226.

Argo, Allison (dir.). 2013. *Parrot Confidential* (film).

Arnold, Amanda. 2020. "The Love Story We All Need Right Now." *The Cut*. https://www.thecut.com/2020/09/my-octopus-teacher-on-netflix-is-the-love-story-we-need.html.

Axelson, Gustave. 2019. "Nearly 30% of Birds in U.S., Canada Have Vanished Since 1970." *Cornell Chronicle*. http://news.cornell.edu/stories/2019/09/nearly-30-birds-us-canada-have-vanished-1970.

Bartal, Inbal Ben-Ami, Jean Decety, and Peggy Mason. 2011. "Empathy and Pro-Social Behavior in Rats." *Science*, 334/6061: 1427–1430.

Bates, Mary. 2014. "The Emotional Lives of Dairy Cows." *WIRED*, June 30.

Beech, Hannah. 2019. "Among Oil Palm, Rain Forest and Orangutan, Shades of Gray." *New York Times*, July 16. https://www.nytimes.com/2019/07/16/reader-center/hope-the-orangutan-indonesia.html.

Bennett, Joshua. 2020. *Being Property Once Myself: Blackness and the End of Man*. Cambridge, MA: Harvard University Press.

Bennholdt-Thomsen, Veronika, and Maria Mies. 2000. *The Subsistence Perspective: Beyond the Globalised Economy*. London: Zed Books.

Berger, John. 1980. "Why Look at Animals?" In *About Looking*. New York: Vintage Books: 3–28.

Bergman, Charles. 2009. "Wildlife Trafficking." *Smithsonian Magazine*. https://www.smithsonianmag.com/travel/wildlife-trafficking-149079896/.

Berlant, Lauren. 2011. *Cruel Optimism*. Durham, NC: Duke University Press.

Bethune, Brian. 2019. "The Mosquito Has Killed Billions and Changed our DNA – and It's Going to Get Worse." *Maclean's*. https://www.macleans.ca/culture/books/mosquito-killed-billions-changed-dna/.

Betz, Adam et al. 2020. "As Coronavirus Loomed, Worthington Pork Plant Refused to Slow Down." https://www.startribune.

com/as-coronavirus-loomed-worthington-pork-plant-refused-to-slow-down/570516612/.

Bittman, Mark. 2011. "Who Protects the Animals?" *New York Times*, April 26. https://opinionator.blogs.nytimes.com/2011/04/26/who-protects-the-animals/.

Blanchette, Alex. 2020. *Porkopolis: American Animality, Standardized Life and the Factory Farm*. Durham, NC: Duke University Press.

Blattner, Charlotte, Sue Donaldson, and Ryan Wilcox. 2020. "Animal Agency in Community: A Political Multi-Species Ethnography of VINE Sanctuary." *Politics and Animals*, 6: 1–22.

Bluefarb, Sam. 1972. *The Escape Motif in the American Novel: Mark Twain to Richard Wright*. Columbus: Ohio State University Press.

Boddice, Rob. 2010. "The Moral Status of Animals and the Historical Human Cachet." *JAC*, 30/3–4: 457–489.

Bong Joon-Ho (dir.). 2017. *Okja* (film).

Brophy, Brigid. 1965. "The Rights of Animals." *Sunday Times*, October 10.

Burt, Jonathan. 2005a. *Rat*. London: Reaktion Books.

Burt, Jonathan. 2005b. "John Berger's 'Why Look at Animals?': A Close Reading." *Worldviews*, 9/2: 203–218.

Butler, Judith. 2006. *Precarious Life*. New York: Verso.

Campos, Marcelo. 2018. "Lyme Disease: Resolving the Lyme Wars." *Harvard Health Blog*. https://www.health.harvard.edu/blog/lyme-disease-resolving-the-lyme-wars-2018061814071.

Care Collective. 2020. *The Care Manifesto: The Politics of Interdependence*. London: Verso.

Carson, Rachel. 1962. *Silent Spring*. New York: Houghton Mifflin.

Cataldi, Susan 2002. "Animals and the Concept of Dignity: Critical Reflections on a Circus Performance." *Ethics & the Environment*, 7/2: 104–126.

Cavell, Stanley. 1979. *The Claim of Reason: Wittgenstein, Skepticism, Morality and Tragedy*. Oxford: Oxford University Press.

Cavell, Stanley. 1976. "Knowing and Acknowledging." In *Must We Mean What We Say? A Book of Essays*. Cambridge: Cambridge University Press: 220–245.

Cecco, Leyland. 2021. "'Heat Dome' Probably Killed 1bn Marine Animals on Canada Coast, Experts Say." *Guardian*, July 8. https://www.theguardian.com/environment/2021/jul/08/heat-dome-canada-pacific-northwest-animal-deaths.

Celermajer, Danielle. 2021. *Summertime: Reflections on a Vanishing Future*. Melbourne: Penguin Australia.

Chamberlain, Lorna, and Rod Preece. 1993. *Animal Welfare and Human Values*. Waterloo, ONT: Wilfrid Laurier University Press.

Church, Russell. 1959. "Emotional Reactions of Rats to the Pain of Others." *Journal of Comparative and Physiological Psychology*, 52/2: 132–134.

Compa, Lance. 2005. "Blood, Sweat and Fear: Workers' Rights in U.S. Meat and Poultry Plants." https://www.hrw.org/report/2005/01/24/blood-sweat-and-fear/workers-rights-us-meat-and-poultry-plants.

Corkery, Michael, and David Yaffe-Bellany. 2020. "Meat Plant Closures Mean that Pigs are Gassed or Shot Instead." *New York Times*, May 14. https://www.nytimes.com/2020/05/14/business/coronavirus-farmers-killing-pigs.html.

Costello, Kimberly, and Gordon Hodson. 2014. "Explaining Dehumanization Among Children: The Interspecies Model of Prejudice." *British Journal of Social Psychology*, 53: 175–197.

Crary, Alice. 2021. "Against 'Effective Altruism'." *Radical Philosophy*, 2.10. https://www.radicalphilosophy.com/article/against-effective-altruism.

Crary, Alice. 2019. "Comments on a Contested Comparison: Race and Animals." In Oskari Kuusela and Benjamin De Mesel, eds., *Ethics in the Wake of Wittgenstein*. London: Routledge.

Darwin, Charles. 1872. *The Expression of the Emotions in Man and Animals*. London: Murray.

D'Eaubonne, Françoise. 1974. *Le Féminisme ou la mort*. Quebec: Femmes en Mouvement.

Debes, Remy. 2009. "Dignity's Gauntlet." *Philosophical Perspectives*, 23: 45–78.

Dengler, Corinna, and Strunk, Birte. 2022. "Feminisms and the Environment." In Luigi Pellizzoni, Emanuele Leonardi, and Viviana Asara, eds., *Handbook for Critical Environmental Politics*. Cheltenham: Edward Elgar Publishing.

Derouin, Sarah. 2019. "Deforestation: Facts, Causes and Effects." *Live Science*, November 6. https://www.livescience.com/27692-deforestation.html.

Derrida, Jacques. 2008. *The Animal that Therefore I Am*, trans. David Wills, ed. Marie-Louise Mallet. New York: Fordham University Press.

Dhont Kristof, Gordon Hodson, and Ana C. Leite. 2016. "Common Ideological Roots of Speciesism and Generalized Ethnic Prejudice: The Social Dominance Human–Animal Relations Model (SD-HARM)." *European Journal of Personality*, 30/6: 507–522.

Diamond, Cora. 2010. "Murdoch the Explorer." *Philosophical Topics*, 38/1: 51–85.

Diamond, Cora. 2001. "Injustice and Animals." In Carl Elliott, ed., *Slow Cures and Bad Philosophers: Essays on Wittgenstein, Medicine, and Bioethics*. Durham, NC: Duke University Press: 118–147.

Donaldson, Sue, and Will Kymlicka. 2011. *Zoopolis: A Political Theory of Animal Rights*. Oxford: Oxford University Press.

Ehrlich, Pippa, and James Reed (dir.). 2020. *My Octopus Teacher* (film).

Ellis, Colter. 2014. "Boundary Labor and the Production of Emotionless Commodities: The Case of Beef Production." *The Sociological Quarterly*, 55/1: 92–118.

Feinberg, Leslie. 2011. "Casualty of an Undeclared War Series." https://transgenderwarrior.org/casualty/.

Ferguson, Sue. 2020. "Women, Work and 'Directly Confronting Capitalist Power': Interview with Sue Ferguson." *A Journal of Texas Marxism*, March 16. https://section44.org/2020/03/16/women-work-and-directly-confronting-capitalist-power-interview-with-sue-ferguson/.

Foot, Philippa. 1985. "Utilitarianism and the Virtues." *Mind*, 94/374: 196–209.

Foster, John Bellamy. 2000. *Marx's Ecology: Materialism and Nature*. New York: Monthly Review Press.

Gaita, Raimond. 2002. *The Philosopher's Dog*. Melbourne: Text Publishing Company.

Garner, Robert, and Siobhan O'Sullivan. 2016. "Introduction." In Robert Garner and Siobhan O'Sullivan, eds., *The Political Turn in Animal Ethics*. London: Rowman & Littlefield International.

Gastanaga, Melvin, Ross C. Macleod, Bennett Hennessey, and Joaquín Ugarte Nuñez. 2010. "A Study of the Parrot Trade in Peru and the Potential Importance of Internal Trade for Threatened Species." *Bird Conservational International*, 21/1: 1–10.

Geuss, Raymond. 1999 [1981]. *The Idea of Critical Theory: Habermas and the Frankfurt School*. Cambridge: Cambridge University Press.

Godfrey-Smith, Peter. 2016. *Other Minds: The Octopus, the Sea, and the Deep Origins of Consciousness*. New York: Farrar, Straus and Giroux.

Godlovitch, Roslind, Stanley Godlovitch, and John Harris, eds. 1971. *Animals, Men and Morals: An Inquiry into the Maltreatment of Non-humans*. London: Victor Gollancz.

Goodall, Jane. 2011. "Jane Goodall's Thoughts on Parrots." *New Life Parrot Rescue.* http://www.nlpr.org.uk/about-nlpr/poems-and-quotes/jane-goodalls-thoughts-parrots.

Gottlieb, Anthony. 2008. "My Parrot, My Self." *New York Times*, October 11. https://www.nytimes.com/2008/10/12/books/review/Gottlieb-t.html.

Goulson, Dave. 2021. *Silent Earth: Averting the Insect Apocalypse*. New York: Harper Collins.

Griffin, Donald. 2001. *Animal Minds: Beyond Cognition to Consciousness*, 2nd edn. Chicago, IL: University of Chicago Press.

Griffin, Donald. 1976. *The Question of Animal Awareness: Evolutionary Continuity of Mental Experience*. New York: Rockefeller University Press.

Griffiths, Paul. 2004. "Instinct in the '50s: The British Reception of Konrad Lorenz's Theory of Instinctive Behavior." *Biology & Philosophy*, 19: 609–631.

Gruen, Lori. 2021. *Ethics and Animals: An Introduction*, 2nd edn. Cambridge: Cambridge University Press.

Gruen, Lori. 2017. "The Moral Status of Animals." In Edward Zalta, ed., *Stanford Encyclopedia of Philosophy*. https://plato.stanford.edu/entries/moral-animal/.

Gruen, Lori. 2014. "Dignity, Captivity, and an Ethics of Sight." In Lori Gruen, ed., *The Ethics of Captivity*. New York: Oxford University Press: 231–247.

Gruen, Lori, and Robert Jones. 2015. "Veganism as an Aspiration." In Ben Bramble and Bob Fisher, eds., *The Moral Complexities of Eating Meat*. New York: Oxford University Press: 153–171.

Guenther, Lisa. 2013. *Solitary Confinement: Social Death and Its Afterlife*. Minneapolis: University of Minnesota Press.

Guy, Clarissa. 2021. "The Other: The Harmful Legacy of Human Zoos." https://www.rmpbs.org/blogs/rocky-mounta in-pbs/the-harmful-legacy-of-human-zoos/.

Hallman, Caspar et al. 2017. "More Than 75 percent Decline over 27 Years in Total Flying Insect Biomass in Protected Areas." *PLOS ONE*, October 18. https://doi.org/10.1371/journal.pone.0185809.

Hare, Richard M. 1999. "Why I am Only a Demi-Vegetarian." In Dale Jamieson, ed., *Singer and His Critics*. Oxford: Blackwell: 233–246.

Harrison, Ruth. 1964. *Animal Machines*. London: Vincent Stuart Publishers.

Herzog, Hal. 2010. *Some We Love, Some We Hate, Some We Eat: Why It's So Hard to Think Straight about Animals*. New York: HarperCollins.

Horkheimer, Max, and Theodor Adorno. 2002. *The Dialectic of Enlightenment: Philosophical Fragments*. Stanford, CA: Stanford University Press.

Hruby, Denise. 2020. "He Once Trafficked in Rare Birds. Now, He Tells How It's Done." *New York Times*, November 27. https://www.nytimes.com/2020/11/27/world/europe/rare-birds-macaws-trafficking-brazil.html.

Hughlett, Mike, and Adam Betz. 2020. "Coronavirus Hit Meat Plants Just as Workers Were Being Ask to Speed Up." https://www.startribune.com/coronavirus-hit-meat-plants-just-as-workers-were-being-asked-to-speed-up/570758212/.

Hunt, Elle. 2020. "*My Octopus Teacher Review*: The Strange Life of Cephalopods Up Close." *New Scientist*, September 7. https://www.newscientist.com/article/2253789-my-octopus-teacher-review-the-strange-lives-of-cephalopods-up-close/.

Jamieson, Dale. 2018. "Animal Agency." *The Harvard Review of Philosophy*, 25: 111–126.

Jamieson, Dale. 1985. "Against Zoos." In Peter Singer, ed., *In Defense of Animals*. Malden, MA: Blackwell: 39–50.

Jamieson, Dale, and Marc Bekoff. 1992. "On the Aims and Methods of Cognitive Ethology." *PSA: Proceedings of the Biennial Meeting of the Philosophy of Science Association*: 110–124.

Jarvis, Brooke. 2019. "How Mosquitos Changed Everything." *The New Yorker*, July 29. https://www.newyorker.com/magazine/2019/08/05/how-mosquitoes-changed-everything.

Jarvis, Brooke. 2018. "The Insect Apocalypse is Here." *New York Times Magazine*, November 27. https://www.nytimes.com/2018/11/27/magazine/insect-apocalypse.html.

Jones, Kendall et al. 2018. "The Location and Protection Status of Earth's Diminishing Marine Wilderness." *Current Biology*, 28/15: 2506–2512.

jones, pattrice. 2019. *VINE Sanctuary News*. https://conta.cc/2KreuXG.

Kagan, Shelly. 2019. *How to Count Animals: More or Less*. Oxford: Oxford University Press.

Kant, Immanuel. 2012 [1785]. *Groundwork on the Metaphysic of Morals*, trans. Mary Gregor and Jens Timmermann. Cambridge: Cambridge University Press.

Kateb, George. 2011. *Human Dignity*. Cambridge, MA: Harvard University Press.

Kim, Claire Jean. 2011. "Moral Extensionism or Racist Exploitation? The Use of Holocaust and Slavery Analogies in the Animal Liberation Movement." *New Political Science*, 33/3: 311–333.

Ko, Aph, and Syl Ko. 2017. *Aphro-ism: Essays on Pop Culture, Feminism and Black Veganism from Two Sisters*. Brooklyn, NY: Lantern Books.

Kolbert, Elizabeth. 2021. *Under a White Sky: The Nature of the Future*. New York: Crown Publishers.

Kolbert, Elizabeth. 2014. *The Sixth Extinction: An Unnatural History*. New York: Henry Holt.

Korsgaard, Christine. 2018. *Fellow Creatures: Our Obligations to the Other Animals*. Oxford: Oxford University Press.

Kotzwinkle, William. 1976. *Dr. Rat*. New York: Marlowe & Company.

Kymlicka, Will. 2017. Review of Robert Garner and Siobhan O'Sullivan, *The Political Turn in Animal Ethics*. *Animal Studies Journal*, 6/1: 175–181.

Kymlicka, Will. 2018. "Human Rights without Human Supremacism." *Canadian Journal of Philosophy*, 48/6: 763–792.

Lazari-Radek, Katarzyna de, and Peter Singer. 2017. *Utilitarianism: A Very Short Introduction*. Oxford: Oxford University Press.

Lazari-Radek, Katarzyna de, and Peter Singer. 2014. *The Point of View of the Universe: Sidgwick and Contemporary Ethics*. Oxford: Oxford University Press.

Legge, Jane. 1969. "Learning to be a Dutiful Carnivore." *British Vegetarian*, Jan/Feb: 59.

Levitt, Tom. 2018. "Dairy's 'Dirty Secret': It's Still Cheaper to Kill Male Calves than to Rear Them." *Guardian*, March 26.

Livingstone-Smith, David. 2011. *Less Than Human*. New York: St. Martin Press.

Lloro, Teresa. 2021. *Animal Edutainment in a Neoliberal Era: Politics, Pedagogy, and Practice in the Contemporary Aquarium.* New York: Peter Lang.

Lockwood, Julie L. et al. 2019. "When Pets Become Pests: The Role of the Exotic Pet Trade in Producing Invasive Vertebrate Animals." *Frontiers in Ecology and the Environment*, 17/6: 323–330.

Loder, Reed Elizabeth. 2016. "Animal Dignity." *Animal Law*, 23/1: 1–64.

Lofting, Hugh. 1988 [1920]. *The Story of Dr. Dolittle.* New York: Yearling.

Longino, Helen. 1990. *Science as Social Knowledge.* Princeton, NJ: Princeton University Press.

Low, Philip et al. 2012. "The Cambridge Declaration on Consciousness." https://fcmconference.org/img/Cambridge DeclarationOnConsciousness.pdf.

Lowen, James. 2021. "Red List Update: Parrots of the Americas in Peril." *BirdLife International*, February 8. https://www.birdlife.org/news/2021/02/08/red-list-update-parrots-of-the-americas-in-peril/.

Lustgartner, Abrahm. 2018. "Palm Oil was Supposed to Help Save the Planet. Instead it Unleashed a Catastrophe." https://www.nytimes.com/2018/11/20/magazine/palm-oil-borneo-climate-catastrophe.html.

Luxemburg, Rosa. 2003 [1913]. *The Accumulation of Capital.* London: Routledge.

Makowska, Joanna, and Daniel M. Weary. 2013. "Assessing the Emotions of Laboratory Rats." *Applied Animal Behaviour Science*, 148/1–2: 1–12.

Maritain, Jacques. 1943. *Christianity and Democracy and The Rights of Man and Natural Law*, trans. Doris C. Anson. San Francisco, CA: Ignatius Press.

Martinez-Alier, Joan. 2002. *The Environmentalism of the Poor: A Study of Ecological Conflicts and Valuation.* Cheltenham: Edward Elgar.

Marx, Karl. 1990 [1867]. *Capital: A Critique of Political Economy,* vol. 1. London: Penguin Books.

McGeer, Victoria. 2004. "The Art of Good Hope." ANNALS of the AAPSS, 592: 100–127.

McMahan, Jeff. 2008. "Eating Animals the Nice Way." *Daedalus,* 137/1: 66–76.

Merchant, Carolyn. 1990. "Preface" to *The Death of Nature,* 2nd edn. San Francisco, CA: Harper & Row: xv–xviii.

Merchant, Carolyn. 1989. *Ecological Revolutions: Nature, Gender and Science in New England.* Durham, NC: University of North Carolina Press.

Merchant, Carolyn. 1980. *The Death of Nature: Women, Ecology, and the Scientific Revolution.* San Francisco, CA: Harper & Row.

Mies, Maria. 1986. *Patriarchy and Accumulation on a World Scale: Women in the International Division of Labour.* London: Zed Books.

Milligan, Tony. 2016. "Putting Pluralism First: Cruelty and Animal Rights Discourse." In Robert Garner and Siobhan O'Sullivan, eds., *The Political Turn in Animal Ethics.* London: Rowman & Littlefield International.

Milligan, Tony. 2015. "The Political Turn in Animal Rights." *Politics and Animals,* 1/1: 6–15.

Milman, Oliver. 2021. "Meat Accounts for Nearly 60% of All Greenhouse Gases from Food Production, Study Finds." *Guardian,* September 13. https://www.theguardian.com/environment/2021/sep/13/meat-greenhouses-gases-food-production-study.

Mitchum, Bob. 2011. "Rats Free Trapped Companions, Even When Given Choice of Chocolate Instead." *uchicago news,*

December 8. https://news.uchicago.edu/story/helping-your-fellow-rat-rodents-show-empathy-driven-behavior.

Mizejewski, David, and David Weber. 2020. "What You Need to Know Before Spraying for Mosquitos." *National Wildlife Federation Blog*, September 2. https://blog.nwf.org/2020/09/what-you-need-to-know-before-spraying-for-mosquitoes/.

Molteni, Megan. 2020. "Why Meat-Packing Plants Have Become Covid-19 Hot Spots." *WIRED*, May 7. https://www.wired.com/story/why-meatpacking-plants-have-become-covid-19-hot-spots/.

Montford, Kelly Struthers. 2016. "Dehumanized Denizens, Displayed Animals: Prison Tourism and the Discourse of the Zoo." *PhiloSOPHIA*, 6/1: 73–91.

Montgomery, Sy. 2015. *The Soul of an Octopus: A Surprising Exploration into the Nature of Consciousness.* New York: Atria Books.

Murdoch, Iris. 1970. *The Sovereignty of Good.* London: Routledge & Kegan Paul.

Nagel, Thomas. 1974. "What Is It Like to Be a Bat?" *Philosophical Review*, 83/4: 435–450.

Nelson, Michael P. 2016. "To a Future without Hope." In Andrew Brei, ed., *Ecology, Ethics and Hope.* London: Rowman & Littlefield.

Nussbaum, Martha C. 2007. *Frontiers of Justice.* Cambridge, MA: Harvard University Press.

Oksala, Johana. 2018. "Feminism, Capitalism, and Ecology." *Hypatia*, 33/2: 216–234, esp. 223–229.

Olah, George et al. 2016. "Ecological and Socioeconomic Factors Affecting Extinction Risk in Parrots." *Biodiversity and Conservation*, 25: 205–223.

Pachirat, Timothy. 2011. *Every Twelve Seconds: Industrialized Slaughter and the Ethics of Sight.* New Haven, CT: Yale University Press.

Parrot Taxon Advisory Group. 2016. EAZA Best Practice Guidelines Ecuadorian Amazon Parrot. https://www.eaza.net/conservation/programmes/#BPG.

Payne, Kate. 2020. "Families of Workers Killed by Covid-19 Sue Tyson Over Waterloo Outbreak." https://www.iowapublicradio.org/post/families-workers-killed-covid-19-sue-tyson-over-waterloo-outbreak.

Pearce, Fred. 2018. "Conflicting Data: How Fast Is the World Losing Its Forests?" *Yale Environment 360*, October 9. https://e360.yale.edu/features/conflicting-data-how-fast-is-the-worlds-losing-its-forests.

Persson, Kirsten, Bernice Simone Elger, and David Martin Shaw. 2017. "The Indignity of Relative Concepts of Animal Dignity: A Qualitative Study of People Working with Nonhuman Animals", *Anthrozoös*, 30/2: 237–247.

Pick, Anat. 2018. "Vegan Cinema." In Emelia Quinn and Benjamin Westwood, eds., *Thinking Veganism in Literature: Toward a Vegan Theory*. London: Palgrave: 125–146.

Pick, Anat. 2015. "Why Not Look at Animals?" *NECSUS*, June 12. https://necsus-ejms.org/why-not-look-at-animals/.

Plumwood, Val. 1993. *Feminism and the Mastery of Nature*. London: Routledge.

Preston, Elizabeth. 2018. "A 'Self-Aware' Fish Raises Doubts About a Cognitive Test." *Quanta Magazine*, December 12. https://www.quantamagazine.org/a-self-aware-fish-raises-doubts-about-a-cognitive-test-20181212/.

Regan, Tom, and Singer, Peter. 1989. *Animal Rights and Human Obligations*. Englewood Cliffs, NJ: Prentice Hall.

Romanes, George. 1892. *Animal Intelligence*. London: Kegan Paul, Trench.

Rosen, Michael. 2012. *Dignity: Its History and Meaning*. Cambridge, MA: Harvard University Press.

Rosner, Hillary. 2018. "The Other Oil Crisis." *National Geographic*, 234/6: 76.

Rowland, Michael Pellman. 2017. "Two-thirds of the World's Seafood is Over-fished: Here's How You Can Help." *Forbes*, July 24. https://www.forbes.com/sites/michaelpellmanrow land/2017/07/24/seafood-sustainability-facts/.

Rueb, Emily S., and Mihir Zaveri. 2020. "How Many Animals Have Died in Australia's Wildfires?" *New York Times*, July 11. https://www.nytimes.com/2020/01/11/world/australia/fires-animals.html.

Ryder, Richard. 1975. *Victims of Science: The Use of Animals in Research*. London: National Anti-Vivisection Society.

Safran Foer, Jonathan. 2009. *Eating Animals*. New York: Little, Brown and Company.

Saldanha, Carlos (dir.). 2011. *Rio* (film).

Salleh, Ariel. 1997. *Ecofeminism as Politics: Nature, Marx and the Postmodern*. London: Zed Books.

Saloner, Brendan et al. 2020. "Covid-19 Cases and Deaths in Federal and State Prisons." https://jamanetwork.com/jour nals/jama/fullarticle/2768249.

Sato, Nobuya, Ling Tan, Kazushi Tate, and Maya Okada. 2015. "Rats Demonstrate Helping Behavior Toward a Soaked Conspecific." *Animal Cognition*, 18: 1039–1047.

Schiermeier, Quirin. 2019. "Eat Less Meat: UN Climate-Change Report Calls for Change to Human Diet." *Nature*, August 8. https://www.nature.com/articles/d41586-019-02409-7.

Schlosser, Eric. 2002. *Fast Food Nation: What the All-American Meal Is Doing to the World*. London: Penguin Books.

Schmitz, Friederike. 2016. "Animal Ethics and Human Institutions: Integrating Animals into Political Theory." In Robert Garner and Siobhan O'Sullivan, eds., *The Political Turn in Animal Ethics*. London: Rowman & Littlefield.

Schulz, Kathryn. 2014. "The Man Who Made Life Shimmer." *Vulture*. https://www.vulture.com/2014/04/schulz-gabriel-gar cia-marquez-obituary.html.

Seibert, Charles. 2019. "Zoos Call it 'Rescue" but Are the Elephants Really Better Off?" *New York Times*, July 9. https:// www.nytimes.com/2019/07/09/magazine/elephants-zoos-swazi-17.html.

Sen, Amartya. 2005. "Human rights and Capabilities." *Journal of Human Development*, 6/2: 151–166.

Singer, Peter. 2015. *The Most Good You Can Do: How Effective Altruism is Changing Ideas about Living Ethically*. New Haven, CT: Yale University Press.

Singer, Peter. 2010. "Speciesism and Moral Status." In Licia Carlson and Eva Feder Kittay, eds., *Cognitive Disability and Its Challenge to Moral Philosophy*. Oxford: Wiley-Blackwell: 331–344.

Singer, Peter. 2009 [1975]. *Animal Liberation*. New York: HarperCollins. See also the 2015 40th Anniversary edn.

Singer, Peter. 1994. *Rethinking Life and Death: The Collapse of Our Traditional Ethics*. New York: St. Martin's.

Singer, Peter. 1979. "Killing Humans and Killing Animals." *Inquiry*, 22/1–4: 145–156.

Singer, Peter. 1972. "Famine, Affluence, and Morality." *Philosophy & Public Affairs*, 1/3: 229–243.

Sorabji, Richard. 1993. *Animal Minds and Human Morals: The Origins of the Western Debate*. Ithaca, NY: Cornell University Press.

Srinivasan, Amia. 2017. "The Sucker, the Sucker!" *London Review of Books*, 39/17. https://www.lrb.co.uk/the-paper/v39/ n17/amia-srinivasan/the-sucker-the-sucker.

Stauffer, Brian. 2019. "'When We're Dead and Buried, Our Bones Will Keep Hurting': Worker's Rights Under Threat in US Meat and Poultry Plants." https://www.hrw.org/

report/2019/09/04/when-were-dead-and-buried-our-bones-will-keep-hurting/workers-rights-under-threat.

Telford, Taylor, and Kimberly Kindy. 2020. "As They Rushed to Maintain U.S. Meat Supply, Big Processors Saw Plants Become Covid-19 Hot Spots, Worker Illnesses Spike." *Washington Post*, April 25. https://www.washingtonpost.com/business/2020/04/25/meat-workers-safety-jbs-smithfield-tyson/.

Thorpe, W.H. 1950. "The Definition of Some Terms Used in Animal Behaviour Studies." *Bulletin of Animal Behavior*, 8: 34–40.

Tinbergen, N. 1963. "On Aims and Methods of Ethology." *Zeitschrift für Tierpsychologie*, 20: 410–429.

Tokarczuk, Olga. 2018. *Drive Your Plow Over the Bones of the Dead*, trans. Antonia Lloyd-Jones. London: Fitzcarraldo Editions.

Tolstoy, Leo. 2009 [1883]. "The First Step." Introduction to Howard Williams, *The Ethics of Diet: An Anthology of Vegetarian Thought*. Guildford: White Crow Books: 11–46.

Uexküll, Jakob von. 1992 [1934]. "A Stroll Through the Worlds of Animals and Men: A Picture Book of Invisible Worlds." *Semiotica*, 89/4: 319–391.

US Department of Interior. 2020. "10 Things Poachers Don't Want You to Know about Wildlife Trafficking." September 9. https://www.doi.gov/blog/10-things-poachers-dont-want-you-know-about-wildlife-trafficking.

Wacquant, Loïc. 2002. "The Curious Eclipse of Prison Ethnography in the Age of Mass Incarceration." *Ethnography*, 3/4: 371–397.

Wadiwel, Dinesh. 2015. *The War Against Animals*. Leiden: Brill.

Waldron, Jeremy. 2017. *One Another's Equals: The Basis of Human Equality*. Cambridge, MA: Harvard University Press.

Waldron, Jeremy. 2013. "The Paradoxes of Dignity: A Review of Michael Rosen, *Dignity: Its History and Meaning.*" *The European Journal of Sociology*, 54/3: 554–561.

Waldron, Jeremy. 2012. *Dignity, Rank and Rights*. Oxford: Oxford University Press.

Warren, Calvin. 2015. "Black Nihilism and the Politics of Hope." *CR: The New Centennial Review*, 15 /1: 215–248.

White, Mel. 2008. "Borneo's Moment of Truth." *National Geographic*, November. https://www.orangutans.com.au/news-the-problem-orangutans-face/borneos-moment-of-truth/.

Williams, Bernard. 1985. *Ethics and the Limits of Philosophy*. London: Routledge.

Williams, Bernard. 1981. "Utilitarianism and Self-Indulgence." In *Moral Luck: Philosophical Papers 1973–1980*. Cambridge: Cambridge University Press.

Williams, Bernard. 1973. "A Critique of Utilitarianism." In J.J.C. Smart and Bernard Williams, *Utilitarianism: For and Against*. Cambridge: Cambridge University Press: 77–150.

Wilson, E.O. 2017. *Half-Earth: Our Planet's Fight for Life*. New York: Liveright.

Winegard, Timothy. 2019. *The Mosquito: A Human History of Our Deadliest Predator*. New York: Dutton.

Wisely, Samantha M., and Gregory E. Glass. 2019. "Advancing the Science of Tick and Tick-Borne Disease Surveillance in the United States." *Insects*, 10/10: 361.

Wissenburg, Marcel, and David Schlosberg. 2014. "Introducing Animal Politics and Political Animals." In *Political Animals and Animal Politics*. London: Palgrave Macmillan: 1–14.

Yang, Gi-geun, Dohyeong Kim, Anh Pham, and Christopher John Paul. 2018. "A Meta-Regression Analysis of the Effectiveness of Mosquito Nets for Malaria Control: The Value of Long-Lasting Insecticide Nets." *International*

Journal of Environmental Research and Public Health, 15/3. https://www.ncbi.nlm.nih.gov/pmc/articles/PMC5877091/.

Zamba, Matthew. 2020. "How Many Animals Are Killed for Food Every Day?" *Sentient Media*. http://sentientmedia.org/how-many-animals-are-killed-for-food-every-day/.

Zuolo, Federico. 2016. "Dignity and Animals." *Ethical Theory and Moral Practice*, 19/5: 1117–1130.

Websites referenced

IUCN 2020. The IUCN Red List of Threatened Species. Version 2020–2. https://www.iucnredlist.org.

https://www.orangutanalliance.org/whats-the-issue/alternative-names-for-palm-oil/.

https://www.npr.org/2018/07/24/631941716/what-its-like-to-be-held-hostage-by-somali-pirates-for-2-1-2-years.

https://www1.nyc.gov/office-of-the-mayor/news/472-17/de-blasio-administration-32-million-neighborhood-rat-reduction-plan#/0.

Foster Parrots. https://www.fosterparrots.com/.

US Department of Interior. https://www.doi.gov/blog/10-things-poachers-dont-want-you-know-about-wildlife-trafficking.

Further Reading

Abrell, Elan. 2021. *Saving Animals: Multispecies Ecologies of Rescue and Care*. Minneapolis: University of Minnesota Press.

Adams, Carol, and Lori Gruen. 2022. *Ecofeminism: Feminist Intersections with Other Animals and the Earth*, 2nd edn. London: Bloomsbury.

Anscombe, G.E.M. 1958. "Modern Moral Philosophy." *Philosophy*, 33/124: 1–19.

Berger, John. 1972. *Ways of Seeing*. London: Penguin.

Boisseron, Bénédicte. 2018. *Afro-Dog: Blackness and the Animal Question*. New York: Columbia University Press.

Bovens, Luc. 1999. "The Value of Hope." *Philosophy and Phenomenological Research*, 59: 667–681.

Cochrane, Alasdair. 2020. *Should Animals Have Political Rights?* Cambridge: Polity.

Colling, Sarat. 2021. *Animal Resistance in the Global Capitalist Era*. East Lancing: Michigan State University Press.

Condon, Matt, and Alice Crary. 2021. "Social Visibility: Theory and Practice." *Philosophical Topics*. https://www.academia.edu/50820179/Social_Visibility_Theory_and_Practice_co_authored_with_Alice_Crary_.

Coulter, Kendra. 2016. *Animals, Work and the Promise of Interspecies Solidarity*. Basingstoke: Palgrave Macmillan.

Crary, Alice. 2018. "The Horrific History of Comparisons Between Animals and Cognitively Disabled Human Beings (and How to Move Past it)." In Lori Gruen and Fiona Probyn Rapsey, eds., *Animaladies*. London: Bloomsbury.

Crary, Alice. 2016. *Inside Ethics: On the Demands of Moral Thought*. Cambridge, MA: Harvard University Press.

Deckha, Maneesha. 2021. *Animals as Legal Beings: Contesting Anthropocentric Legal Orders*. Toronto: University of Toronto Press.

Deckha, Maneesha. 2018. "Postcolonialism." In Lori Gruen, *Critical Terms for Animal Studies*. Chicago, IL: University of Chicago Press.

Dordoy, Alan, and Mary Mellor. 2000. "Eco-socialism and Feminism: Deep Materialism or the Contradictions of Capitalism." *Capitalism, Nature, Socialism*, 11/3: 41–61.

Foot, Philippa. 2001. *Natural Goodness*. Oxford: Oxford University Press.

Foster, John Bellamy. 2000. *Marx's Ecology: Materialism and Nature*. New York: Monthly Review Press.

Gaard, Greta, ed. 1993. *Ecofeminism: Women, Animals, Nature*. Philadelphia, PA: Temple University Press.

Gillespie, Kathryn. 2018. *Cow with Ear Tag #1389*. Chicago, IL: University of Chicago Press

Glick, Megan. 2018. *Infrahumanism*. Durham, NC: Duke University Press.

Gruen, Lori. 2018. *Critical Terms for Animal Studies*. Chicago, IL: University of Chicago Press.

Gruen, Lori. 2015. *Entangled Empathy: An Alternative Ethic for Our Relationship with Animals*. Brooklyn, NY: Lantern Books.

Gruen, Lori, and Fiona Probyn Rapsey, eds. 2018. *Animaladies*. London: Bloomsbury.

Guenther, Lisa. 2012. "Beyond Dehumanization: A Post-Humanist Critique of Intensive Confinement." *Journal for Critical Animal Studies*, 10/2: 47–68.

Hribal, Jason. 2011. *Fear of the Animal Planet: The Hidden History of Animal Resistance*. Chico, CA: AK Press.

Jackson, Zakiyyah Iman. 2020. *Becoming Human: Matter and Meaning in an Antiblack World*. New York: New York University Press.

Jenkins, Stephanie, Kelly Struthers Montfort, and Chloe Taylor. 2020. *Disability and Animality: Crip Perspectives in Critical Animal Studies*. New York: Routledge.

jones, pattrice. 2014. *Oxen at the Intersection*, Brooklyn, NY: Lantern Books.

Kelly, Robin. 2003. *Freedom Dreams: The Black Radical Imagination*. Boston, MA: Beacon Press.

Kheel, Marti. 2008. *Nature Ethics: An Ecofeminist Perspective*. Lanham, MA: Rowman & Littlefield.

Kim, Claire Jean. 2018. "Abolitionism." In Lori Gruen, ed., *Critical Terms in Animal Studies*. Chicago, IL: University of Chicago Press.

Kim, Claire Jean. 2015. *Dangerous Crossings: Race, Species, and Nature in a Multicultural Age*. Cambridge: Cambridge University Press.

Livingstone-Smith, David. 2021. *Making Monsters: The Uncanny Power of Dehumanization*, Cambridge, MA: Harvard University Press.

Marceau, Justin. 2019. *Beyond Cages: Animal Law and Criminal Punishment*. Cambridge: Cambridge University Press.

Montford, Kelly Struthers, and Chloe Taylor, eds. 2020. *Colonialism and Animality: Anti-Colonial Perspectives in Critical Animal Studies*. New York: Routledge.

Morgan, Jennifer. 2004. *Laboring Women: Reproduction and Gender in New World Slavery*. Philadelphia: University of Pennsylvania Press.

Murdoch, Iris. 1997. "Vision and Choice in Morality." In *Existentialists and Mystics: Writings on Philosophy and Literature*. New York: Penguin Books: 76–98.

Perkins, Patricia Ellie. 2013. "Environmental Activism and Gender." In Deborah Figart and Tonia Warnecke, eds., *Handbook of Research on Gender and Economic Life*. Cheltenham: Edward Elgar Publishing: 504–521.

Robinson, Cedric. 1983. *Black Marxism: The Making of the Black Radical Tradition*. Chapel Hill: University of North Carolina Press.

Radford Ruether, Rosemary. 1975. *New Woman/New Earth: Sexist Ideologies and Human Liberation*. New York: Seabury.

Salleh, Ariel. 1988. "Epistemology and the Metaphors of Production: An Eco-Feminist Reading of Critical Theory." *Studies in the Humanities*, 15/2: 130–139.

Sharpe, Christina. 2016. *In the Wake: On Blackness and Being*. Durham, NC: Duke University Press.

Sturgeon, Noel. 1997. *Ecofeminist Natures: Race, Gender, Feminist Theory and Political Action.* New York: Routledge.

Taylor, Sunaura. 2017. *Beasts of Burden: Animal and Disability Liberation*. New York: The New Press.

Whyte, Kyle Powys, and Chris J. Cuomo. 2017. "Ethics of Caring in Environmental Ethics: Indigenous and Feminist Philosophies." In Stephen Gardiner and Allen Thompson, eds., *The Oxford Handbook of Environmental Ethics*. Oxford: Oxford University Press: 305–322.

Index